BRITAIN IN OLD PHO

Around Hoyland
A Second Selection

GEOFFREY HOWSE

SUTTON PUBLISHING LIMITED

Sutton Publishing Limited
Phoenix Mill · Thrupp · Stroud
Gloucestershire · GL5 2BU

First published 2000

Title page photograph: Hoyland Law Stand,
6 May 1935. Local residents pose by the
bonfire built to mark Hoyland's final event of
the Silver Jubilee celebrations for their
Majesties King George V and Queen Mary.
The bonfire, built mostly of old pit-tubs and
planking, was lit at 10 p.m. by Cllr J.L. Joyce
JP, Chairman of Hoyland UDC. Such bonfires
or beacon fires were often lit on special
occasions on Hoyland Law, which rises to a
height of 593 ft. (*Sandra Hague collection*)

British Library Cataloguing in Publication Data
A catalogue record for this book is available from the
British Library.

ISBN 0-7509-2726-7

Typeset in 10.5/13.5 Photina.
Typesetting and origination by
Sutton Publishing Limited.
Printed and bound in England by
J.H. Haynes & Co. Ltd, Sparkford.

Viscount Milton, aged seven, at the garden
party held at Wentworth for soldiers'
comforts, 22 August 1918 (see also page
101). (*Sandra Hague collection*)

CHARLES . EDWARD . ELLIS .

CONTENTS

The Strafford Arms Inn, seen here during the closing years of the nineteenth century. (*Sandra Hague collection*)

A late Edwardian view of West Street, featuring the Princess Theatre, built in 1893. (*Sandra Hague collection*)

The Church of England Mission Hall, Hoyland Common, opened on 14 April 1884 and seen here *c.* 1910. This building later became St Peter's Parish Hall. (*Sandra Hague collection*)

INTRODUCTION

In this second selection of old photographs of Hoyland and the surrounding area, I have included some subjects and districts I was unable to cover in my first book. Such is the diversity of material available locally and the overwhelming amount of supporting historical information that I have found it very difficult to select images from the many photographs offered to me; I have been spoilt for choice. In order to create a balance between factual information regarding the background of some of the subjects and the development of various communities, I have included some anecdotal information.

In addition to the photographs and engravings I included in *Around Hoyland*, I also collected a great deal of surplus material, which has paved the way for this second book. Having read *Around Hoyland*, many people have very generously offered photographs, documents and other information, which has helped me considerably; and for their assistance I am most grateful.

Since the publication of *Around Hoyland* I have been told stories about how a place got its name or why a particular building was built. For instance, one amusing story was told by a genial migrant to Platts Common, whose roots lie far beyond the Hoyland township. Despite this fictional account, he passed on some useful information to me regarding events that had taken place since he had lived in the locality. He clearly had been well versed in the story he related and genuinely believed the story of how Elsecar got its name to be fact. As is usually the case, regardless of the century the story has supposedly stemmed from, it involved Earl Fitzwilliam. Exactly which earl is not clear, but what is apparent is that in the minds of many Yorkshire people any male member of the illustrious families who resided at Wentworth Woodhouse is invariably named Earl Fitzwilliam: there have been six holders of that title resident in the area since 1782, their predecessors, holding the titles of Marquess of Rockingham, Earl of Strafford and, in the case of earlier Wentworths, baronet and knight. The story goes that Earl Fitzwilliam was in love with a lady who fell off her horse and broke her neck, while riding in what is now the village of Elsecar. The lady's name was none other than Elsie Carr. So it came to pass that the Earl was so distraught that he named the village in her honour. This is just one of many such stories concerning place names, monuments and miscellaneous places and events which follow a similar pattern in the telling, and which delight many people. Despite irrefutable evidence to the contrary, such stories continue to be told.

As I have been repeatedly asked where the information came from for *Around Hoyland* and other books, I would like to satisfy the curiosity of my readers. I began researching Hoyland Nether and Wentworth, in particular, when I was a student at Barnsley School of Art, in 1973. I spent many hundreds of hours in the local studies department at the old library in Barnsley Civic Hall and Sheffield Central Library, where the Fitzwilliam Manuscripts were then kept. I was also given considerable help by the late O.W. Carr, Estate Agent to the 10th Earl Fitzwilliam. The encouragement I received during my early research spurred me on and I have continued to research diverse subjects ever since.

In 1975, I went to London, where I spent three years training as an actor at Mountview Theatre School, which included a course at the National Film School. However, I did not entirely neglect my research, and would often spend my spare time visiting historical sites, churches, graveyards and cemeteries. I also wrote poetry and was encouraged by the then Poet Laureate, Sir John Betjeman. Over a considerable number of years, I have accumulated pamphlets, books, documents, maps, paintings, engravings and photographs; collected in London, Yorkshire, the United States of America, and throughout the United Kingdom and Ireland, during numerous prolonged periods of touring with plays and musicals, both as an actor and impresario. I have spent many hours in archives, libraries and country houses, gathering information and assimilating facts gleaned from knowledgeable individuals I have been fortunate enough to meet.

In 1992 I began writing for the long-established theatrical magazine *Plays & Players*. In addition to writing regular columns, I also wrote mini-biographies, conducted interviews and reviewed theatrical productions, in the Fringe, West End, provinces and abroad, and for some time was also restaurant critic. I continued to research subjects in South Yorkshire and as a result of my efforts was commissioned to write two books in this series, *Sheffield in Old Photographs* (published 1997) and *Doncaster in Old Photographs* (published 1998). I was also commissioned to write two further books on Sheffield, *A Century of Sheffield* (published 1999) and *Sheffield Past and Present* (published 2000).

It is also important to consider the contribution made by other authors and historians. Other people's works provide, at the very least, useful pointers to where information can be obtained. I am constantly coming across articles which have been lifted directly from the pages of the work of Arthur K. Clayton, without any reference or acknowledgement. Mr Clayton, who is now at the age of ninety-nine, still dispensing acts of kindness, spent over three-quarters of a century researching subjects in South Yorkshire. His contribution in assisting future generations of historians is incalculable. I have referred to his work on numerous occasions and I would be the first to admit that I owe a debt of gratitude to him. Among the many documents and books I have referred to I have found some useful information in Sheila Margaret Ottley's *While Martha Told the Hours*, Clarence Walker's *A Glance Over My Shoulder*, Michael Bedford's *Hoyland Nether Through The Years* and Charles Twigg's *Village Rambles*.

It is only possible to produce books such as this if visual material is available. On no fewer than three occasions during the writing of this book, I have spoken to people in Hoyland who have told me that they have lost their entire collection of old photographs because they have been destroyed by a family member. One lady was particularly distraught by this, as her son had told her that he didn't want them and they would only be burned when she died anyway. A relative of mine whose wife has no room for sentiment was extremely upset when he discovered that his wife had deliberately destroyed his boyhood photographs when she needed some extra cupboard space. He was devastated by this, and commented, 'More than half of my life has gone there.' I would strongly urge the readers of this book to ensure that any photographs they have in their possession are carefully labelled and dated, wherever possible, so that in the years to come, there can be no doubt about their origins.

I would also suggest that readers should try to instil in their families the importance of preserving photographic records. If old photographs are not wanted don't throw them away. Offer them to an archive, library, museum or private collector, so that they might be put to good use in the future. Every day somebody's past is being consigned to the rubbish tip and important artefacts are being irretrievably lost.

As far as I am aware, I have included the most up-to-date research material concerning the various subjects in this book. I have made every effort to research each individual photograph, in an attempt to establish exactly who or what appears in it. Sometimes it has not been possible. I apologise unreservedly for any errors or omissions. Some of the views I have expressed stem from my personal observations and I accept that the reader may disagree with some of my assertions.

Geoffrey Howse, November 2000

1

Hoyland Nether &
Hoyland Common

John Knowles Memorial Church, Free Church of England, seen here shortly after its completion in 1912. (*Sandra Hague collection*)

King Street, Hoyland, *c.* 1905. With the exception of Ottley's draper's shop (now Thawley's newsagents), their house (whose chimneys can be seen beyond) and part of the Co-op drapery store, all the buildings seen here have been demolished. (*Sandra Hague collection*)

King Street from just below Ottley's draper's (as seen above), *c.* 1900. Many of the buildings seen here remain today, but those on the immediate right have long since vanished from the Hoyland townscape. (*Sandra Hague collection*)

St Peter's Church and vicarage, *c.* 1900. (*Sandra Hague collection*)

Kirk Balk Cemetery opened in 1924, after the neighbouring churchyard of St Peter's and the extension opposite the church, in Hawshaw Lane, became full, owing to Hoyland's rapidly increasing population. This view of the cemetery gates was taken shortly after the cemetery opened. The Latin inscription reads 'death is the gateway to everlasting life'. (*Walker's Newsagents collection*)

The ceremony held in High Street, on 20 September 1911, to lay two foundation stones for the John Knowles Memorial Church, Free Church of England. Seen on the platform is the Right Rev. William Troughton, Bishop Primus of the Free Church of England, and Mrs Elizabeth Bartlett (sister of John Knowles), who laid the foundation stones. (*Sandra Hague collection*)

The ceremonial mallets and trowels presented to Bishop Troughton and Mrs Bartlett, on the occasion of the laying of the foundation stones for John Knowles Memorial Church. (*Sandra Hague collection*)

Edward Robinson, landlord of the Five Alls, King Street, Hoyland, poses outside his pub, 1890s. (*Sandra Hague collection*)

Edward Robinson poses outside the Five Alls with members of the Hague family, during the Edwardian period. The engraved glass window was added after the coronation of King Edward VII. The King is depicted centre top. The characters who appear in the window are a soldier (I fight for all), a king (I rule all), a judge (I plead for all), a gentleman (I pay for all) and a bishop (I pray for all). The Five Alls ceased to be a public house shortly before the Second World War. It became a private residence and remained so until the entire building was demolished in 1973 (see page 26). (*Sandra Hague collection*)

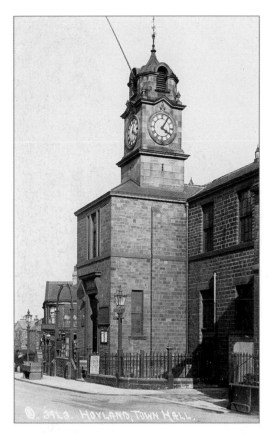

Hoyland Town Hall, *c.* 1905. (*Sandra Hague collection*)

The clocktower, which housed 'Old Martha', a clock named after its donor, Martha Knowles, was a prominent landmark in Hoyland, situated on top of Hoyland Town Hall. It is seen here being taken down shortly after the Town Hall closed on 11 June 1973. The stones were carefully numbered before they were put into storage, as the intention was to rebuild the clocktower on a new site in Hoyland. (*Courtesy of Edwin Hugh Stenton and Amy Stenton*)

Market Street, *c*. 1905. On the right, the large double-fronted house on the corner of Spring Gardens is Brentwood, no. 46. This house was built for Herbert Garner in the late Edwardian period. Herbert Garner owned the ironmonger's shop at 22 High Street. After Garner's premature death in 1932, Lichie Walker took over his business premises, and since then Garner's former shop has traded as Walker's Newsagents. (*Sandra Hague collection*)

The laying of the foundation stone at the Miners' Welfare Hall, King Street, Hoyland, by Thomas Tomlinson (later Sir Thomas), 13 October 1923. In the background can be seen King Street School and beyond, on the Elsecar border, the Electra Palace Cinema. (*Sandra Hague collection*)

Jack Whitehouse on duty in King Street, 1939. (*Margaret Gaddass collection*)

Ernest Allen (piano), Arnold Firth (drums) and Walter Whitehouse (trumpet and vocals) appear at the Strafford Arms during the 1940s. (*Margaret Gaddass collection*)

Hoyland UDC councillors and staff, 1950. Included in the photograph are W.G. Danks, H. Hague, T. Butterworth, C. Jones, E. Coult, G. Hazel, H. Fieldsend, L. Steeples, K. Barraclough, J. Shepherd, D. Chadwick, A. Laister, G. Clarke, E. Kield, A.E. Wilkinson (Chairman), N. Mell, V. Houlton and D. Eaden. (*Courtesy of Edwin Hugh Stenton and Amy Stenton*)

King Street and High Street, mid-1960s. (*Walker's Newsagents collection*)

For over three-quarters of a century the name Wiggins was closely associated with the treatment of the sick in Hoyland. Dr Barclay Wiggins (1867–1959) was born in Ayrshire. Having completed his medical training at St Mungo's College, University of Glasgow, he qualified in 1893 and a fortnight later was appointed assistant to a doctor in Bacup, Lancashire. In 1894 he came to Hoyland as assistant to Dr William Ritchie. In 1914 Dr Wiggins began to practise on his own. For nearly twenty years he worked without a holiday, until he was joined by his son Dr Albert William Barclay Wiggins (1903–85) and Dr John Aitken McEwan. Dr Barclay Wiggins was, until a few months before his death at the age of ninety-four, still visiting patients, usually on foot, often walking as much as 6 miles. In an interview on his ninetieth birthday he said: 'I don't think I can give a better recipe than hard work and plain living.' He also confessed: 'Of course I don't work as hard as I used to, and I don't have any night calls.' He added: 'If I had my choice again, I wouldn't be anywhere other than in Yorkshire; I have always liked Hoyland.' In the photograph, taken in the 1950s, Molly is seated next to her master Dr Barclay Wiggins. His son, Dr A.W. Barclay Wiggins, sits on the bench next to him, which is outside Thistle House, the Wiggins' family home. (*Courtesy of Mary Dickerson*)

A gathering of members of Hoyland & District Newsagents in the 1950s, with guests from the National Federation of Retail Newsagents. Back row, left to right: Geoff Walker, Federation guest, Sid Shaw, Alf Ellaway, Federation guest, Lichie Walker. Front row: Avis Walker, Mabel Shaw, Mrs Ellaway, Annetta Walker. (*Courtesy of Mabel Shaw and Sue Jenkins*)

A dinner held at the Strafford Arms in the late 1960s to mark the retirement of Brian Keys, who was manager of the Yorkshire Bank and also ran the local office of the *South Yorkshire Times*. Many local businesses were represented at the dinner. Back of table: Les Webster (Webster's Furnishing, Hoyland Common), Joan Masheder, Ted Masheder (Milton Motor Co.), Lennie Roberts, bank manager, Percy Charlesworth, Dorcas Charlesworth, Alf Ellaway and Mrs Ellaway (newsagents), Mr Asquith and Mrs Asquith (fruiterers, Hoyland Common). Seated at the extreme top right of the photograph: Brian Keys. Front of table: David Walker, Christine Walker (Walker's Newsagents), Derek Bean (antiques dealer and furniture restorer), Jessie Matsell (draper, Hoyland Common) and George Taylor (Taylor's electrical shop). (*Walker's Newsagents collection*)

Staff and pupils at West Street Infants' School, popularly known as the 'Sunshine School' on account of its glazed walkways, 1955. On the right is schoolmistress Mrs Ashby and on the left the headmistress Mrs Kathleen Magson. (*Joan Masheder collection*)

This mid-1950s view of West Street Infants School shows pupils building shapes and models. (*Joan Masheder collection*)

One of T. Burrows & Sons' coaches enters High Street, Hoyland, 1960. It is just passing Guest's butcher's shop, on the left. It is interesting to note the 'bobby' on the beat, a familiar sight in Hoyland until the middle of the following decade; a far cry from today's pitiful police presence in Hoyland and district. (*Joan Masheder collection*)

Hoyland & District Burns Club, First Annual Supper, held at the Strafford Arms on Monday 25 January 1965. The address to the haggis was given by A.W. Cuthbertson, which was followed by the Selkirk Grace. Chairman K.W. Pate gave the welcome and diners sat down to supper, consisting of cock-a-leekie soup, haggis with mashed neeps and champit tatties, or stirk pie, champit tatties and green peas, followed by apple pie and cream, or bannock and kebbuck, and coffee. The immortal memory was given by T. Halliday. H. Goddard, chairman of Hoyland Chamber of Trade, proposed the toast, on behalf of town and trade, and Cllr Jack Ashmore, chairman of Hoyland UDC, gave the reply. Artistes appearing were Miss J. Ferris and Mr B. Swift. In the photograph the haggis is piped into the concert room at the Strafford Arms. (*Joan Hopson collection*)

Kirk Balk School, 1963. Kenneth Masheder, aged fourteen, puts the finishing touches to his occasional table in the woodwork class. (*Joan Masheder collection*)

A view of Bank Corner and Market Street from Hoyland Town Hall in 1970, photographed by Ted Masheder during the festive season. The annual Christmas tree, which for many years stood on the same site, adjacent to the Strafford Arms, was anchored to a large iron ring – which had once served to tether elephants when, according to information supplied by Joan Hopson, former landlady of the Strafford Arms, they visited the area with a travelling circus. On the right the single-storey building in the Market Place, just beyond Hoyland cinema, is the popular café and sweet shop, run by Mrs Helen Kelly, who was sometimes assisted by her husband, Albert. The Kellys later moved across the road to larger premises, known as the Wishing Well Café. Behind the café are the snow-clad rooftops of St Andrew's Parish Hall, formerly the National Hoyland Infants' School (1854–1934), which closed after West Street Infants' School opened in 1934 (see page 18), and beyond it is the large gable of Wainwright's, off-licence, tobacconist, confectioner and general store. (*Joan Masheder collection*)

Opposite, bottom: Milton Road, Hoyland, during winter 1964, photographed by Ted Masheder from just below his family's bungalow. With the exception of a recently built detached house, constructed where the open gateway can be seen on the left, very little has changed in over thirty-five years. (*Joan Masheder collection*)

Looking from George Street across to Hall Street and beyond, November 1970. On the right is the snooker hall run by the half-brothers Arthur McDonald and Enoch Peach. This much missed Hoyland establishment was popularly known as the 'dog hole' or in local parlance, 't' dog 'oil'. The building became structurally unsafe and remained empty for several years, before it was replaced by a new building of similar proportions after Southgate had been created, but its proposed re-opening as a snooker hall didn't happen. The building was eventually converted into single-storey dwellings. Southgate now cuts across the area covered by grass and shrubs. (*Joan Masheder collection*)

Looking across George Street from the t' dog 'oil, 1971. Kelly's Terrace, situated in High Croft (formerly Dick Croft), can be seen on the right. (*Joan Masheder collection*)

There was great excitement caused by the re-opening of Hoyland Market on 24 October 1970, on its temporary site behind the old Town Hall. Hundreds of people came to support it and ensure its success. (*Joan Masheder collection*)

A group of shoppers watch with interest as a market trader offers his wares at bargain prices, 24 October 1970. Two youngsters in the photograph are Philip Mann and Martin Horsefield. (*Joan Masheder collection*)

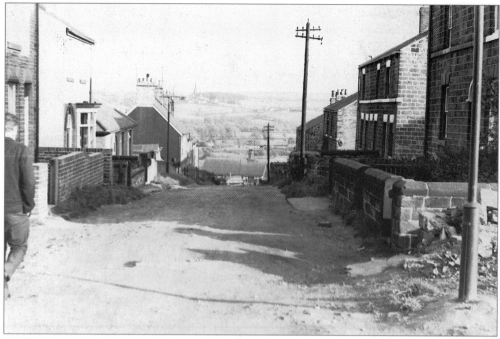

George Street, 1971. The houses on the right were demolished during the redevelopment of Hoyland town centre. (*Joan Masheder collection*)

Looking in the opposite direction, also 1971. (*Joan Masheder collection*)

A view across High Street from High Croft, 1970. The former Melias store is occupied by the Decorating Centre. Frank Vickers is still trading as Storey & Cooper. That shop was split into two single-storey shops, and part of the rear portion and the entire first floor of both Storey & Cooper and the former Melias store were converted into flats, utilising the original stone-built Holly House to the front of which the brick-built shops were added in 1927. Melias' former store is now occupied by the Identity dress shop, and Storey & Cooper's by J. Hall & Sons greengrocer's and the Hoyland Garden & Pet Centre. (*Joan Masheder collection*)

Kirk Balk School from Hoyland war memorial, winter 1970. (*Joan Masheder collection*)

Southgate, 1988, with the Masheders' bungalow on the left. The Kwik Save supermarket on the right occupies part of the site of Masheder's Garage. The land in between the supermarket and the bungalow, which included over two-thirds of the Masheders' garden, was compulsorily purchased by Hoyland Nether UDC to allow the Southgate development to take place. The Gate Inn can be seen on the left, behind the Masheders' bungalow. The building on the right is the Ball Inn. (*Joan Masheder collection*)

Looking towards King Street from what is now Southgate, 1973. Here the house, which was once the Five Alls, which closed in the 1930s (see page 11), is being demolished. (*Courtesy of Edwin Hugh Stenton and Amy Stenton*)

The Hague family has long been established in Hoyland, and records show that William Hague of Hoyland purchased land in Jump in 1777. William died on 10 March 1810; his wife Anne died on 17 June in the same year, and was buried at Wentworth. In his will, William's sons, Joseph and Isaac, were the main beneficiaries. Isaac Hague, farmer and nailmaker, died on 20 November 1852, and left his land in Jump and the residue of his estate to his wife Sarah. He hoped that Earl Fitzwilliam would allow his wife and family to remain in the homestead. This homestead, known as Kirk House, is situated at 112 Market Street. Isaac's will also directed that his son, also called Isaac, should remain there after his wife's death. Earl Fitzwilliam did indeed allow the Hague family to remain in Market Street. Isaac Hague, farmer and stonemason, died on 15 November 1883, without making a will. His eldest son, John, a miner of Jump, put the Hague land at Jump and two dwellings into trust, with John Knowles, gentleman, of Hoyland Nether, and George Guest, butcher, of Platts Common, to sell on behalf of the family. The mineral rights were to remain with the Hague family. Isaac Hague had nine children living at that time: the aforementioned John, Albert (stonemason, Elsecar), Thomas (stonemason, Hemingfield), Mark Arthur (stonemason, Hoyland Nether), Lucy (spinster, Hoyland Nether), Henry (pupil teacher, Hednesford, Staffordshire) and Edward, Isaac and George. As the last four children were all minors, the monies raised by the trustees were to be invested on behalf of Sarah, mother of the children and the deceased Isaac's wife, and after her death the residue was to be divided equally among the children.

James Arthur Hague, Marian Hague and Mark Arthur Hague outside Kirk House, *c.* 1923. (*Sandra Hague collection*)

Mark Arthur Hague, farmer and stonemason, who lived at Kirk House, 112 Market Street, died on 27 December 1935. His son Arthur, of 8 George Street, Hoyland, and his daughter Doris, who was living at Kirk House, were executors of his will. Arthur was bequeathed considerable property in Hoyland and Hoyland Common, as were Doris and his other daughters. Shortly after Mark Arthur's death, his daughter Doris acquired Rose Cottage, Duke Street, Hoyland, and Arthur Hague moved into Kirk House. This should not be confused with Kirk Farm, which stood in Market Street until the middle of the twentieth century, on the site of what is now St Andrew's Community Centre. The farmhouse of Kirk Farm was built end on to Market Street, and its paddock occupied the site where three pairs of semi-detached houses were built, between Brentwood and St Andrew's Church.

The 7th Earl Fitzwilliam sold the land farmed by the Hagues, which was bounded by Royston Hill, Hawshaw Lane, Kirk Balk and Market Street, for the building of a council estate, which was erected in 1937. Arthur Hague bought the entire homestead, which included Kirk House, the cottages, farm buildings and barns, from Earl Fitzwilliam's Wentworth Estates for £1,000. Arthur and his two sons, James Arthur and Harold, then concentrated on the building side of their business, Arthur and his wife Doris living in Kirk House and his sons in adjoining properties. Compensation relating to the mineral rights from the land in Jump was distributed among numerous members of the Hague family after Newman and Bond, the family's solicitors, informed Arthur on 2 December 1939 that they had completed matters regarding the removal of coal by the colliery company. By August 1946 all accounts relating to the future removal of coal on that land were finalised, as when the coal industry was nationalised in 1947 all mineral rights came to an end.

Arthur Hague and his labourer, c. 1925. (*Sandra Hague collection*)

James Arthur Hague (on the plough) and his labourer, 1920s. Kirk House can be seen in the background on the right. (*Sandra Hague collection*)

Arthur Hague died on 1 January 1959. Some of the property connected to the original homestead, including Kirk House, was sold several years later. James Arthur Hague died in 1976, and his wife Iris died in 1998, leaving a daughter, Sandra (born 1955). Harold Hague died in 1999.

The Hague family has played an important role in many aspects of Hoyland life for well over two centuries, and for the last hundred years or so many members of the family have been closely associated with building. There are still many Hague family members living around Hoyland today.

James Arthur Hague, his wife Iris (née Bedford) and their daughter Sandra in the garden of Kirk Cottage, 1959. (*Sandra Hague collection*)

Building the Primitive Methodist Church, Hoyland Road, Hoyland Common, which opened for worship on 23 May 1903. In the photograph are Tom Hague (wearing the bowler hat) and Mark Hague. (*Sandra Hague collection*)

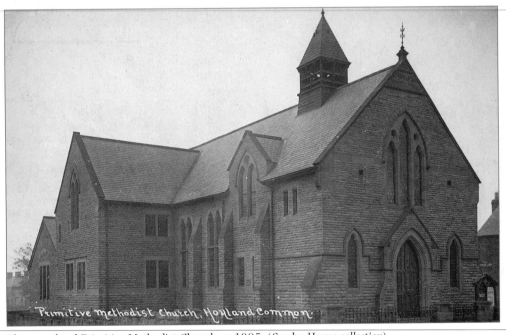

The completed Primitive Methodist Church, *c.* 1905. (*Sandra Hague collection*)

he Primitive Methodist Church, *c.* 1935. The stones have taken on the blackened appearance characteristic of 1e majority of stone buildings in the area. The shop, at the top of Stead Lane, was occupied during that period by .W. Hardy, who ran it from 1930 to 1938. Hoyland Common Primitive Methodist Church was demolished in July 970. (*George Hardy collection*)

family group at the home of Mary Alice Vaines, 43 Allott Street, Hoyland Common, 1927. Left to right: Lily rst (née Hardy), Mary Alice Vaines (née Hardy), Elizabeth Wheeler (née Hardy) and Kate Hardy (née Hall). *eorge Hardy collection*)

Stuart and Kenneth Masheder, aged four and five respectively, in the garden of the family home, 8 Skiers View Road, Hoyland Common, 1955. Ted and Joan Masheder had this detached house built to their specifications by the building firm Corbett's. Building commenced in 1950. Shortly after the bricks had been laid and the roof was on the Masheders' new home Mr Corbett went to France and his business was declared bankrupt. The Masheders were faced with a partly finished house without electricity, floorboards or plaster. This was during the period when wood could only be purchased on licence. The only wood they could obtain was some bastard redwood, which was very expensive. The difficulties the Masheder encountered getting their new home completed prompted them to name it The Blandings, after the film of the same name which starred Greer Garson and Walter Pidgeon. The plot of the story centred on a dream house that new owners bought and attempted to renovate: major problems ensued. Despite a shaky start the Masheder family lived at The Blandings from 1951 until 1961, after which they moved to a bungalow, built by the well-known Elsecar firm W. Chadwick and Son, on a plot adjacent to Masheder's Garage in Milton Road, Hoyland. In the photograph Stuart is feeding one of the cows from Plumes Farm (Fearnley Grove Farm), whose farmhouse and land is currently occupied by Fearnhouse Crescent and part of the Cloughs Estate. The cow was a regular visitor to the Masheders' garden, as was a black sheep which used to come begging for food every day. The sheep became very attached to Mrs Masheder, and one day, when she was going downstairs, she met the sheep coming up the stairs to meet her. On more than one occasion the sheep followed her to Mrs Otterwell's shop, on the corner of West Bank and Vernon Street. (*Joan Masheder collection*)

Joan Masheder, on the left, with her cousin Gladys Summers, on the front porch of The Blandings, 1951. (*Joan Masheder collection*)

Hoyland Road, Hoyland Common, 1970. This shows the green by the old people's bungalows, where Hoyland Nether UDC erected the annual Christmas tree. (*Joan Masheder collection*)

Sheffield Road, Hoyland Common, 1970. A potential customer looks at goods on offer in the window of Fearon's pet shop. All the buildings seen in this photograph remain today. (*Joan Masheder collection*)

Looking up Skiers View Road, Hoyland Common, from Stead Lane, 1970. The Elsecar firm W. Chadwick and Son are well under way with building work on their bungalows at the top of Cloughfields Road. (*Joan Masheder collection*)

Parkside Road, Hoyland Common, from Stead Lane, winter 1970. This photograph is taken from the same spot as the one above, but looking in the opposite direction. (*Joan Masheder collection*)

2

Platts Common

The Union Hotel, Barnsley Road, Platts Common, 1960s. (*George Hardy collection*)

Platts Common lies just within the north-east boundary of Hoyland township with Wombwell. Joseph Dickinson' map of 1750 has the name Platts written across the area which is now Barnsley Road and Wombwell Road, jus before the roads leave Hoyland township and join up with the townships of Worsborough and Wombwell. I William Fairbank's survey of Hoyland township, in 1771, the uninhabited and enclosed Platts Common amounte to an area covering just over 33 acres. After the Hoyland Enclosure Act of 1794, as one of the commons i Hoyland it was divided and allotted to Francis Edmunds, George Oates, F. Lundy, Wm Wordsworth, Thos Shaw an the executors of Samuel Phipps. In 1801 George Gillott, woodman, of Hoober Stand, and John Gillott, patter maker, of Sheffield, bought 10 acres of land called Birchen Hills and Owler Close in Upper Hoyland. This land wa just to the west of the border of the enclosed Platts Common. An entry in St Peter's Church register of 185 shows the baptism of William, the son of George and Ann Gillott of Platts Common. Research undertaken by Pete Marsh suggests that these Gillotts may have been members of the family who had 10 acres of land in Uppe Hoyland in 1802, and that the Gillotts then lived at Platts House, which stood on part of the site where the Roya Oak public house stands today. Further evidence of this is indicated by a later sale of land in 1842, which becam the site of the Hoyland Silkstone Colliery.

A presentation outside the Royal Oak, by the Mayor of Barnsley, Cllr Ted Galvin (mayor from May 1980 to Apri 1981), of cheques to Hoyland charities. Featured in the photograph are members of the Blue Lights, a fund-raising organisation connected to Hoyland Ambulance Station, and members of the charities involved. Collecting cheque on behalf of their charities are Joan Masheder and Philip Ackroyd. (*Joan Masheder collection*)

hree separate transactions recorded in the West Riding Registry of Deeds in 1837, 1838 and 1839 concern an state covering 102 acres in the townships of Hoyland and Worsborough. The transactions covered the sale of and by the Earl of Mulgrave, of Mulgrave Castle, to William Vizard, of Lincoln's Inn Fields. Part of the estate had nce belonged to Samuel Phipps, also of Lincoln's Inn Fields (who was mentioned in the Hoyland Enclosure Act of 794). He had bought his portion of the estate in 1779, when Francis Townend, the largest landowner in oyland after the Marquess of Rockingham, sold the entire Townend Estate. The 102 acre Vizard estate included pper Blacker Farm (Blacker Grange) and Hoyland Hall, tenanted by Henry Hartop (a partner in the Milton onworks and later manager of Earl Fitzwilliam's Elsecar Ironworks), who lived there from the 1820s, until 1841. he estate remained in the control of the Vizard family for over forty years. Arthur K. Clayton has established that ne William Vizard who purchased the estate in Hoyland was the same William Vizard who acted as attorney to ueen Caroline during her trial in 1820. He died at Little Faringdon, Berkshire, in 1859, in his eighty-fifth year. Iis son, also called William, inherited the estate but did not long survive his father. He died in 1865 and the state passed to his brother, the Rev. Henry Brougham Vizard, who died at the age of forty-nine in 1874, when he estate passed to his son, Harry William Vizard of Portland Place, Lyme Regis, Dorset – its last Vizard owner. He ut the estate up for sale in 1884.

Ioyland Hall, during the early twentieth century. This attractive late-Georgian building described on page 25 of Around Hoyland may have stood on the site of an earlier hall, although there are indications that the Hoyland Hall eferred to in some documents is probably Upper Hoyland Hall, which certainly has much older origins than the building standing at the end of Market Street. (Hoyland Hall has now been enlarged and is an old people's home.) *Sandra Hague collection*)

Hoyland Silkstone Colliery, early 1900s. (*Sandra Hague collection*)

In 1840 the estate's first Vizard owner, William, purchased 6 acres of coal under Hoyland Common. In th
same year he exchanged 40 acres of coal under the land at Fearnley Grove Farm, near West Bank, Hoyland
with some coal under Platts Common and the 'Lowe'. This land belonged to the 5th Earl Fitzwilliam. Willian
Vizard's intention was to sink a mine, named the Hoyland and Elsecar Coal Company, and transport coal t
Elsecar Canal by an inclined railway from his mine at Platts Common. In 1842 he bought 9¾ acres of Barnsle
thick coal, lying under Upper Hoyland, from Thomas Gillott, carpenter, of Hoyland. Indications are that th
was the same parcel of 10 acres that had been purchased by George and John Gillott in 1802, minus the ¼ acr
plot where Platts House once stood: this was where the Royal Oak stands today. By 1844 miners at Mr Vizard
pit (the name by which the mine was referred to locally) were on strike, in order to obtain an eight-hou
working day.

ousing in Platts Common was slow to develop, and by 1871 the only buildings there were Gillott's Cottages
nd a few houses opposite them. Mr Wells, a partner in the company of Wells, Birch and Ryde who were lessees
 the pit at that time, promised to build further houses and a chapel when a new 20 ft diameter mine shaft was
nk in 1874. This shaft reached the Silkstone seam of coal at a depth of 510 yd. The lessors of the coal were
ainly the 6th Earl Fitzwilliam and the Rev. Henry Vizard (who died in the year the new shaft was sunk). In
877 a branch line, about a mile in length, connected the Hoyland Silkstone Colliery with the main line, the
uth Yorkshire Railway. Following the closure of Elsecar and Milton Ironworks in 1884, sales of coal dropped.
s the Vizard estate derived its income primarily from coal, Harry Vizard put the entire estate up for sale with a
serve price of £20,000. The Vizard estate had grown a little and comprised 124 acres, including Hoyland Hall,
acker Grange Farm, Hawshaw Lane Farm, Hawshaw Cottage and eleven other freehold cottages. The Hoyland
lkstone Colliery was also on the estate, and in the previous three years the rent and royalty payments had
nounted to between £1,500 and £1,600 per annum. The highest bid for the estate was just £10,000, so it was
ithdrawn from sale. In the years that followed business at the colliery was bad, and Mr Fincken, an official
quidator, managed its affairs, during which time it was constantly in danger of closure; then in 1888 the
lliery itself was offered for sale by auction. By 1898 the colliery, now owned by Hoyland Silkstone Coal and
oke Co. Ltd, employed 1,290 men and boys underground and 360 on the surface. During the colliery's last
ars of coal production the Hoyland company was amalgamated with Newton Chambers and Co. Ltd, who
osed the colliery in 1928. Two of the pit shafts were filled in but the main shaft was in regular use for letting
wn and winding up some of the miners from Rockingham Colliery. The site of Hoyland Silkstone Colliery is
ow occupied by Platts Common Industrial Estate.

oyland Silkstone Colliery, mid-1920s. The colliery closed in 1928. (*Walker's Newsagents collection*)

Looking towards Platts Common from the junction of Hawshaw Lane and Market Street, winter 1970. (*Joan Masheder collection*)

Super Suits Ltd, constructed on the fringes of Platts Common Industrial Estate, seen here from Wombwell Road, mid-1970s. (*George Hardy collection*)

3

Upper Hoyland &
Shortwood

Typical cottages in the hamlet of Upper Hoyland, 1960s.
(*Courtesy of Ivy Conway*)

Upper Hoyland, 1880s. The lady wearing the long dress and apron on the left has been tentatively identified as Mrs Blanche Wood, mother of one of the twentieth century's much-loved Upper Hoyland matriarchs, Granny Gibson, who lived at 139 Upper Hoyland Road, in the left foreground. On the right-hand side, above 122 Upper Hoyland Road and beyond the gate, are steps which lead down to a well. In the background on the right are the New Row cottages. (*Sandra Hague collection*)

The hamlet of Upper Hoyland, or Over Hoyland as it is referred to in many accounts, and on numerous documents during and prior to the nineteenth century, is inextricably linked with the Townend family, at one time the largest landowners in the Hoyland township excepting the owners of the enormous estate attached to Wentworth Woodhouse. Available evidence suggests that the Townend family, who eventually settled in Upper Hoyland, may have originated in Worsborough: a member of the family paid taxes there in the year 1567. In 1605 Richard Townend died, leaving in his will, dated 1 January 1605, two properties and land at Upper Hoyland. He also left 10s per year to the poor of Upper Hoyland, 20s per year to the poor of Nether Hoyland, and 40s per year (rent from one of the houses at Upper Hoyland) for the poor of Worsborough. At his death his estate was valued at £1,000, his income having derived from 'setting sprents for birds' (traps) and 'getting candle rushes' (rushlights). These lights were made from rushes gathered during summer, which were then soaked, stripped and bleached. They were then covered in scalding hot fat or grease. Rushlights were the only affordable means of artificial lighting in the homes of the poorer classes. In 1632 Thomas Townend left his houses and land at Upper Hoyland to his son and heir Richard, and bequeathed Stead Farm to his younger son Thomas. This farm had been purchased from a Mrs Watts of Wortley. According to Thomas' will, his wife Jane was to run the farm and ensure that the profits from Stead Farm were used to educate their son Thomas until he 'came of age in his twenty-third year'. A coal mine near Stead Farm was to be worked by Thomas' eldest son Richard, and after a year a third of the profits would go to his mother, Jane. This mine would have been small, possibly employing just three or four hewers. Arthur K. Clayton, in *Hoyland Nether*, mentions that these mine workings were rediscovered in 1957, when open-cast mining uncovered the Barnsley bed seam. In 1634 the Townend family purchased more land in the Hoyland area from Lewis West, Archdeacon of Carlisle. The family's wealth had increased considerably, with land owned around Stead Farm, Upper Hoyland Hall, Hawshaw Lane, Blacker Grange, Woodhouse Farm (West Street, Hoyland), Fork Royds (at the end of Market Street) and at Hoyland Law (where old mine workings were found during open-cast mining). The Townends also owned Woodhead Farm, Wombwell.

Parish Church Schools, Hoyland.

oyland Law School, *c.* 1895. The turret of the Law Stand can be seen to the right of the school building, hind the tree. This school was one of many such establishments which educated Hoyland's children. Hoyland harity School, Lane End (1725–1801), was situated near where Booth's clothing factory now stands, and jacent to Lane End Farm. After its closure as a school it became a cottage (demolished during the last quarter the twentieth century), and was replaced by larger school premises. This school, Hoyland Charity School 810–38), which once stood on Market Street at its junction with Mell Avenue, on the site of what remains day of the once attractive Festival Gardens. The old school building in Market Street existed until 1949. Since closure as a school it has served a number of purposes, including a meeting place, until the 5th Earl tzwilliam, the owner of the property, had it converted into a dwelling in 1850. It remained a house until 1928, d was last used by the Salvation Army. When they vacated the premises the building stood empty until it was molished. Hoyland Law School (1838–1934), seen here, opened immediately after the closure of the Market reet School, with George Armitage as its schoolmaster. In 1842 the school's pupils consisted of seventy-five ys and twenty-three girls. In 1850 the 5th Earl Fitzwilliam donated £35 10s for building work at the school, d a further £51 7s in 1851. In 1862 a new classroom was added, paid for by a National Society grant and onies from the trustees of George Ellis of Brampton. Like his father before him, the 6th Earl Fitzwilliam ntinued to support the school, at the time known as Hoyland Law National School, and helped with building sts in 1866 with a donation of £27 10s for mason's work at the school and schoolhouse. In 1872 his Lordship so paid £10 8s for a new water pump. Hoyland Law School continued to educate Hoyland's children, but after ing placed on a blacklist by the Board of Education in 1925, it continued on a downward spiral. In 1933 its der pupils went to the nearby newly opened Kirk Balk School after the summer holidays. The younger children tended for a further year, until in 1934 the school closed. The building was used for a time by St Peter's urch as a Sunday school. After it fell into disrepair the building was demolished in December 1939. Today a ingalow stands on the site. (*Sandra Hague collection*)

Hoyland Law School, 1902. (*Sandra Hague collection*)

Now well established in the area, Richard Townend (see page 42) was made Chief Constable of the Wapentake of Strafford and Tickhill in 1659. He died in 1688 at the age of eighty-one. In his will, dated 4 January 1683, he left a large house at Upper Hoyland, which had eight hearths recorded on the Tax Roll of 1672 and also a flour parlour and brewing room. It is most likely that this was Upper Hoyland Hall, which at the time was worth £593 9s 4d. Richard's wife Jane died in 1709 aged seventy-nine. They had three sons and four daughters, all of whom lived long lives, and it was their children who built the chapel at Hoyland Law in about 1720.

Arthur K. Clayton was responsible for researching the history of the Townend family. In his initial investigations he helped to remove turf from several Townend memorials, which lie within the ruined nave of Wentworth Old Church. Hoyland's residents were usually buried at Wentworth, and a charge of 1d was levied for taking bodies over estate land. One such charge was applied to people using Burying Lane, which passed through the Skiers Hall estate.

In 1722 Joshua Townend of Stead Farm, son of Richard Townend, bequeathed 4 sellions (unenclosed parcels of land) in Law Side Field to St Peter's Chapel. He left Stead Farm to his godson Richard Malin. This bequest was disputed by Joshua's two daughters, Anne and Jane Townend, but they were unsuccessful in their law suit on 21 November 1726. On 16 January 1732 Thomas Townend, who had inherited the Townend estates from his father, Richard, in 1688, died aged seventy-three and was buried in the nave of Wentworth Old Church. Like his father before him, Thomas had become Chief Constable in 1703. Thomas's sister Anne, who died at the age of seventy-one, was also buried there, in August of the same year. Thomas left the bulk of his estate to his brother Richard and his sister Elizabeth. He left £40 each to his brother Francis, to Francis's son Richard and daughter Sarah. It seems that Francis lived at Blacker, as it is recorded that Francis Townend of Worsborough paid taxes of 8s in 1708. The aforementioned Anne Townend, who died in 1732, left her house and land at Kendal Green, Worsborough, to her brother Richard, with the condition that rent from properties be given to the chapel at Hoyland, when consecrated. Richard had himself given a farm at Benn Bank, Dodworth, and £200 towards the living at Hoyland Chapel. Richard Townend of Upper Hoyland died in 1743, and was buried in the south-west corner of Hoyland Chapel yard, which had been consecrated on 19 November 1740. He bequeathed all money due to him on bonds and other securities to his sister, Elizabeth Walker of Worsborough, to pay off debts of £500. Most of his estate went to his nephew Richard, son of his brother Francis. Elizabeth Walker lies in the same grave as her brother Richard, and Francis lies nearby. Francis' gravestone bears a coat of arms, and describes him as 'Gent late of Blacker died 13 December 1754 aged 88'.

Upper Hoyland treat, 20 July 1907. (*Sandra Hague collection*)

In 1750, the year the 1st Marquess of Rockingham died, he had just completed a 'tower on Hoyland Law'. Hoyland Law Stand was built as a hunting lodge on one of the highest points in the area. It commanded a fine view over the surrounding countryside. Tankersley Park, owned by Lord Rockingham, had a fine herd of red deer, and the Townend family had a pack of stag hounds. In 1751 Charles, 2nd Marquess of Rockingham, appointed Richard Townend Master of Game in 'My Manor of Hoyland'. From this time the fortunes of the Townend family of Upper Hoyland went into rapid decline. The reason may never be discovered, but somehow Richard Townend ran into debt of spectacular proportions. In 1763 he mortgaged Hawshaw House, the Fork Royds and two houses. This debt must have been repaid because in 1765 he mortgaged Hawshaw House again, along with Blacker House. In 1765 and 1766 he was taken to court for debts totalling £4,083. Richard died in 1766, with his affairs in disarray, leaving his wife Anne (née Milner, of the Old Hall, Rockley), together with their son Francis and five daughters. Richard's will had been drawn up in 1753, and Mr Fenton, the attorney, was to assist Anne in sorting out her husband's affairs and looking after the future of the children. There are strong indications that some of the smaller parcels of land owned by the Townend family were handed over to pay debts. This could account for the large number of small freeholders whose names appear on documents concerning the Hoyland area in the years that followed. Woodhead Farm and its land in Wombwell were sold to Elizabeth Tofield in 1769. In 1781 Francis took control of what remained of the Townend estate, which still consisted of 338 acres of land in the Hoyland district. Francis was ordered to sell the estate to pay off creditors by a decree in the Court of Chancery dated 21 February 1776, and in 1779 the sale of the Townend estate in Hoyland was announced in the *London Gazette*. This marked the end of the once influential Townend family in Hoyland.

Many of the buildings in Upper Hoyland which stand today would have been recognisable to the Townends, particularly those connected with farming. The 1603 enclosure of lands act mentions six husbandmen at Upper Hoyland, an indication that there were possibly six farms here at the time. This was later reduced to four, and in the early twentieth century the farms worked were Upper Sycamore Farm (the Birk family), Upper Hoyland Hall (the Lodge family), Lower Sycamore Farm (the Calvert family) and High Royd Farm (the Hudson family). Today Upper Hoyland's working farms have been reduced to two, Lower Sycamore Farm and High Royd Farm.

Three Upper Hoyland girls on a visit to Cleethorpes, 1937. Left to right: Phoebe Bennett, Rita Chambers, Grace Hurst. (*Courtesy of Mrs Phoebe Duggan*)

Phoebe Bennett of Upper Hoyland married Alfred Duggan of Clydach, Swansea, at St Helen's RC Church, Hoyland, on 4 September 1945. The happy couple are seen here cutting the wedding cake outside 139 Upper Hoyland Road, the home of Miss Bennett's grandmother, Granny Gibson. (*Courtesy of Mrs Phoebe Duggan*)

No. 139 Upper Hoyland Road, winter 1947. The black cocker spaniel was called Rover and belonged to Granny Gibson. (*Courtesy of Mrs Isabelle Gillick*)

Blanche Gibson (1889–1961), a kindly lady who was known affectionately as Granny Gibson, outside her home in 1950. (*Courtesy of Phoebe Duggan*)

Granny Gibson with her great-grandchildren in 1952. Left to right: David Gillick, Jean Gillick, Brian Gillick Granny Gibson nursing baby John Bennett, Sandra Bennett and Carole Bennett. (*Courtesy of Phoebe Duggan*)

A gathering in New Row, *c.* 1954. Back row, left to right: Mrs Hazelwood, John Senior, Gordon Hazelwood, Peter Senior. Front row: Grace Hague, Barbara Hazelwood, Melvin Conway, Keith Hazelwood, Derek Addley. (*Courtesy of Ivy Conway*)

Upper Hoyland residents, 1950s. Included in the photograph are Rita Chambers, Mrs Andrews, Grace Hague and Joan Chambers. (*Courtesy of Ivy Conway*)

Upper Hoyland from Hoyland Law Stand, 1960s. (*Courtesy of Ivy Conway*)

One of Upper Hoyland's well-known residents, who lived at 6 Upper Hoyland Road in the 1970s, '80s and until her death on Monday 16 August 1999, was Miss Williamina Kennedy Dunnett OBE, MA. Miss Dunnett graduated from Edinburgh University in 1933 and became an assistant mistress at Thorne Girls' School, near Doncaster. In 1946 she moved to Kirk Balk School, Hoyland, as headmistress of the Girls' School. When Kirk Balk School became co-educational in 1962 Miss Dunnett stayed on as headmistress. The school was extended, and in 1967 became a comprehensive school, which at one time had over 1,600 pupils. In the New Year's Honours List of 1975 Miss Dunnett was awarded the OBE for her outstanding work in education. In 1976 she retired, and was presented with a mounted gold sovereign and chain by Sir Alec Clegg, Chief Education Officer of the former West Riding County Council. After her retirement Miss Dunnett took a keen interest in supporting local church and community activities. Although in later years she became less mobile, she kept her intellect and charm to the end. Miss Dunnett is seen here in about 1970 at the retirement party for the school gardener, Dick Moody (holding tankard), which was held at the Queens Head. Miss Dunnett is on the right, wearing glasses and a string of pearls. Also featured in the photograph are Tom Fuller (caretaker), Martin Monkhouse (assistant caretaker), Mrs Mavis Foster (who made a cake for the occasion in the shape of a wheelbarrow), Horace Blythe, Mrs Moxon, Mrs Whitehouse, Mrs Mary Burgin, Mrs Dora Eltham (head cook), Mrs Lomas, Mrs Francis Marchant, Mrs Maud Copley, Mrs Kay, Mrs Joan Clayton and Mrs Lily Parkin.

Hoyland Brick Co., Shortwood, *c.* 1923: workers pose outside one of the kilns. Among those seen here are: Harry Taylor, Joe Sanderson, Punch Sykes, Norman Oldfield, Frank Money, Lauder Green, Joe Tollerfield, Gus Thompson, Frank Gardner, Ernest Ward, Murny Clark, Stan Jepson, Harry Green, Irving Jepson, Lofty Vickers, Albert Blackburn, Henry Lodge, Tich Kay, John Jepson, Shaw, Ward and Alvie. (*Courtesy of Peter Marsh and Margaret Marsh*)

A little further down the lane from Upper Hoyland is the area known as Shortwood, which lies between High Royd Farm and Short Wood. On a map of 1860 there is a tannery shown, situated near High Royd Colliery: Arthur K. Clayton's *Hoyland Nether* states that 'at the Mechanics Institute in Hoyland, on 30 April 1859, James Russell, farmer and tanner of High Royd Hill Farm, said that he had been a Liberal since 1807'. The tannery was located to the north of the main hamlet, so that the smell of the tanyard would not cause offence to the locals: the skins were initially soaked in solutions that contained all manner of unpleasant things, including urine and the dung from hens, pigeons and dogs, and then in solutions of oak bark. Both Short Wood and Singleton Wood contained oak trees and these may have supplied the necessary raw material. The tannery must have closed sometime between 1859 and 1879, because in the diary of a Mr Herbert Lax it is recorded that 'A new brickworks commenced at Shortwood Old Tanyard on 8 May 1879.' This was operated by Messrs Chambers and Dawson. A huge quarry was dug to provide clay for the brickworks. In 1957 the works became a subsidiary of Thomas Marshall and Co. Ltd of Loxley, who re-named it Hoyland Marshall. During its later years the firm was taken over by G.R. Stein Refractories Ltd. The 100 ft chimney was used up to 1971, but in 1973 it was struck by lightning and demolition followed in September 1974. By the 1990s the brickworks were working with a limited staff, and by 1998 they had closed.

Shortwood Villas FC, 1933. (*Courtesy of Peter Marsh and Margaret Marsh*)

The landscape surrounding Upper Hoyland has changed several times over the last few hundred years. Most recently the brickworks have gone and the waste heap of Rockingham Colliery has been removed; this happened when RJB Mining outcropped any remaining coal. The newest feature to scar the landscape has been the Dearne Valley link road, which has cut off the cottages at Shortwood from Upper Hoyland. An agricultural bridge links the farmland, but if the residents of Shortwood wish to go to Hoyland they no longer have access through Upper Hoyland, and have to use the link road. In the past many of Upper Hoyland's residents would have been connected with farming or mining, but today they are mostly either retired or commuters. If the proposed Shortwood Industrial Zone and the extension to Platts Common Industrial Estate materialise, further changes, perhaps not beneficial, could occur in this small community.

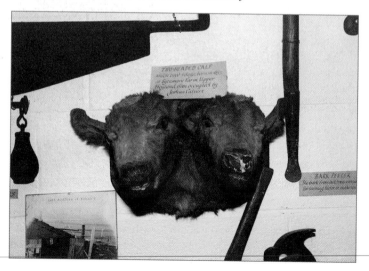

The stuffed remains of the two-headed calf (now an exhibit at the Victoria Jubilee Museum, Cawthorne), born in 1853 at Lower Sycamore Farm, which was then occupied by Joshua Calvert. The calf lived for four days. (*Courtesy of Peter Marsh*)

4

Elsecar

One of Elsecar's familiar sights from the mid-nineteenth century, engine no. 3, an 0–4–2 tender engine, built in 1849, and named Fitzwilliam. The 5th Earl was chairman of the South Yorkshire Doncaster and Goole Railway Company, formed by Act of Parliament in 1847. The first trains ran on the South Yorkshire Railway, as it became known, in November 1849. In 1850 the Elsecar branch of the South Yorkshire Railway opened, and the first coal to be carried to Doncaster was in a train of twenty wagons, carrying 6½ tons each. (*Courtesy of Les Gaddass*)

The Barley Corn, one of Elsecar's many vanished public houses. It was situated in Stubbin (Hill Street) just below the Fitzwilliam Arms. This photograph probably dates from between 1881 and the early 1900s. The property was converted into two houses and last occupied by Mr and Mrs Leathers and Mr and Mrs Baker. The buildings seen in the photograph became severely dilapidated and were demolished by Hoyland UDC, during the period when many old buildings throughout the area were pulled down. (*Courtesy of Edwin Hugh Stenton and Amy Stenton*)

The Milton Arms, seen here on the left during the late nineteenth century, when the entrance was in Armroyd Lane. In the background is the Miners' Lodging House, built by the 5th Earl Fitzwilliam in 1850. (*George Hardy collection*)

Miss Caroline Howe, headmistress of Elsecar Girls' School, in the late Victorian period. Miss Howe retired in 1926. (*Courtesy of Edwin Hugh Stenton and Amy Stenton*)

A general view of Elsecar from Millhouses Street, 1890s. Wagons, with the letters MR painted on their sides, can be seen in the goods/shunting yard of the Midland Railway Company. Many of the buildings connected to Elsecar station had not yet been built. (*George Hardy collection*)

Fitzwilliam Street, early 1900s. (*George Hardy collection*)

Fitzwilliam Street, early 1900s. The Butchers Arms, another of Elsecar's vanished pubs, can be seen at the bottom of the street as it bends to the left. The pub occupies the part of the building to the left, directly behind the gas lamp. Today this old pub, now a private house, is easily recognisable because of its exterior dark green tiles. (*George Hardy collection*)

A garden party at Elsecar Vicarage, early 1900s. Among those present were the following. Standing: W. Walker, G. Jackson Hicks, Mrs D. Belk, Miss Caroline Howe, Miss Coulson, M. Allott, Mrs V. Utley. Seated: D. Kennedy, Mr Lichfield, Mrs L. Winter, Mr and Mrs W. Winter, Mrs T. Walker, Mrs A. Chapman, Miss M.B. Booth and the Rev. Charles Molesworth Sharpe. (*Courtesy of Edwin Hugh Stenton and Amy Stenton*)

Empire Day celebrations at Elsecar Church of England Girls' School, 1906. (*Courtesy of Edwin Hugh Stenton and Amy Stenton*)

Elsecar's celebrated Newcomen-type engine in operation. (*Courtesy of Carl Swift*)

A photograph taken from the same spot in the 1980s. The gigantic hangar-like building on the left was constructed by the NCB. Its presence alongside some of the village's most historic buildings spoils and disfigures the entire area. (*Courtesy of Carl Swift*)

he car carrying their Majesties King George V and Queen Mary, leaves the Elsecar workshops, 9 July 1912. A
oup of onlookers stand outside Earl Fitzwilliam's private railway station (built in 1870). (*Sandra Hague collection*)

he Hospital Festival held by Elsecar and Hoyland Hospital Movement, 18 May 1918. (*Courtesy of Edwin Hugh*
enton and Amy Stenton)

Elsecar Church of England Girls' School, c. 1908. The girls are Madge
Gale and Norah Utley. (*Courtesy of Edwin Hugh Stenton and Amy Stento*

Elsecar Church of England Girls' School, 1913. Minnie Turne
and Doris Johnson are pictured. (*Courtesy of Edwin Hugh
Stenton and Amy Stenton*)

Elsecar Church of England Girls' School, 1913. Nora Utley i
seated: she became a schoolmistress and ended her teachin{
career as senior mistress at Kirk Balk School. In the centre
Martha Howse, daughter of William and Martha Howse of
1 Wentworth Road. She married Ron Taylor and they move
to Strafford Place, Thorpe Hesley. On the right is Kathleen
Hollings. (*Courtesy of Edwin Hugh Stenton and Amy Stenton*)

secar reservoir, *c.* 1920. (*Courtesy of Edwin Hugh Stenton and Amy Stenton*)

he Low Wood, early twentieth century. (*Courtesy of Edwin Hugh Stenton and Amy Stenton*)

Elsecar from Beacon Fields, *c. 1922.* (*Walker's Newsagents collection*)

Elsecar from the same spot as the previous view, photographed by Paul T. Langley Welch in July 1999. In the Elsecar valley the most noticeable change is the disappearance of the cupola chimney and the two gas-holders. Where there were once fields, behind the spire of Holy Trinity Church, today there are houses. (*Author's commission*)

The Bible class outside Elsecar Church of England Boys' School, 1930s. Back row, left to right: Whittaker, Walker, Hicks, Goodaire, Gray. Middle row: Watson, Chadwick, Hough, Bamforth, Purslow. Front row: Elden, Waring, Gray, Pumphery, Sands, Morrell, Hunter. (*Courtesy of Edwin Hugh Stenton and Amy Stenton*)

A nativity play at Elsecar Congregational Church, Hill Street, 1930s. Those featured include Reg Bamforth, Mr Scott, Dorothy Power, Mr Noble, Mary Naylor, Mr Foy, Edwin Moody, Miss Ottley, Jean Sellers, Iris Bamforth, Sheila Dewhurst, Joan Howse, Betty Hardwick, Master Hague, Miss Ottley, Iris Howse, Winnie Cuttings and Mary Adams. (*Courtesy of Keith and Joan Bostwick*)

The family of Samuel D. Smith, landlord, outside the Crown Inn, 1926/7. In the photograph are Mrs Smith, Mary Smith (later Whitehouse), Horace Smith and Percy Smith. (*Margaret Gaddass collection*)

The May queen and attendants pose outside Holy Trinity Church, 1932. In the photograph are Misses E. Wheeler, M. Ostcliffe, M. Shaw, P. Portman and P. Brown and the Vicar, the Rev. James Vesey Roome. (*Margaret Gaddass collection*)

A group of children in the yard of the Market Hotel, *c.* 1935. Back row, left to right: Gordon Davy, Jack Howse, Alan Thickett, Joseph Howse. Front row: Colin Haigh, Joan Howse, Iris Howse, Margaret Taylor, Michael Thickett. The dog on the left was called Patch. (*Courtesy of Iris Ackroyd*)

A group of Elsecar residents pose for a photograph in the back yard of the Market Hotel during celebrations marking the Silver Jubilee of their Majesties King George V and Queen Mary, 6 May 1935. Among those present at the celebration were Mrs Clara Thickett, Horace and Gladys Thickett, Mr Jack Clark and Mrs Edith Clark, Mr and Mrs Radley and their daughter and son in law Mr and Mrs Saxby, Mr Isadore Howse and Mrs Clara Susannah Howse, Miss Sarah Howse, Miss Martha Howse, Miss Edith Howse, Miss Iris Howse, Miss Joan Howse, Herbert Howse, Jack Howse and Mr and Mrs Littelby. (*Doreen Howse collection*)

ARP wardens in the playground of King Street School, 1939. Standing, left to right: G.H. Jackson (head warden), P.C. Sanders (instructor), F. Hinchcliffe, F. Hague. Seated: M. Sanders, W. Harrison, B. Doyle. (*Courtesy of Edwin Hugh Stenton and Amy Stenton*)

ARP wardens in the playground of Elsecar Church of England Girls' School, 1939. Back row, left to right: B. Walton, W. Watts, H. Bamforth, R. Bamforth, J. Drury. Middle row: H. King, E. Haywood, T.H. Hardy, E. Drury, C. Greenfield, E. Turner, G. Littlewood. Front row: M. Roystone, C. Hough, D. Hague, R. Hill, W. Rivers. (*Courtesy of Edwin Hugh Stenton and Amy Stenton*)

One of the popular Newsagents' Dances, held at the Milton Hall, Elsecar, 1940s. Among the revellers are many of the area's business and professional residents. They include Arthur Hague, Dorothy Hague, Mr and Mrs Taylor, Fay Bassindale, Letty Meakin (music teacher from Kirk Balk School), Joyce Fletcher, Claire Massingham, Dr Whitelaw, Sally Bamforth (formerly Miss Sarah Howse), Mrs Parkin, Mary Parkin, Mr and Mrs Armitage, Mrs Armstead and Sid and Mabel Shaw. (*Courtesy of Mabel Shaw and Sue Jenkins*)

A group of Elsecar schoolchildren pose in the playground before their dray leaves to join a parade. Unfortunately I have been unable to find out anything further about the event that is being celebrated, and it has not been possible to give a date or put names to faces. It is such a lovely photograph that I thought it was worth including. It appears to depict King Henry VIII, Cardinal Wolsey, and other characters of the Tudor period. (*Courtesy of Edwin Hugh Stenton and Amy Stenton*)

Elsecar Gas Works was erected in 1857 and operated by the Elsecar Gas Company. The Stenton family has bee
closely associated with Elsecar Gas Works since it first opened, and members of the Stenton family still live at th
former Gas House (the name by which the elegantly proportioned house was known locally) at 8 Wath Road, see
here. A partially full gas-holder can be seen behind the house. The eighteenth-century chimney behind the gas
holder, which pre-dates the gas works by more than sixty years, was originally a cupola chimney, which extracte
air from the mine shaft at Elsecar New Colliery, and was later used by the mine to provide a ventilation system. I
was used by Elsecar Gas Works as an exhaust for the steam boilers, to stop water in the gas-holders freezing, an
for the steam-driven pumps. William Stenton was engineer and manager of the gas works until 1927, when h
son Edwin replaced him. Sheffield and District Gas Company eventually took over the company, and from th
1930s gas was piped to Elsecar from Sheffield. Elsecar Gas Works was nationalised in 1947; thereafter Ea
Midlands Gas Board continued to supply coal gas to the Elsecar works, where it was purified. The works late
became a storage and distribution centre and remained so until the mid-1960s, when the piping of North Sea ga
to the area made the works redundant.

Edwin Stenton was born in 1904. After Elsecar Gas Works closed, and until his retirement at the age of sixty
six, he became superintendent at Sheffield Gas Works and assistant area engineer at Wombwell, Swinton, Wath
upon-Dearne and Barnsley. He retired when North Sea gas replaced coal gas throughout South Yorkshire. Afte
the Elsecar Gas Works was partly demolished, leaving the house and several useful buildings, such as the offic
and various storage facilities, Edwin was able to purchase the house and all the remaining buildings on the ¾ acr
site for £500. (*Courtesy of Edwin Hugh Stenton and Amy Stenton*)

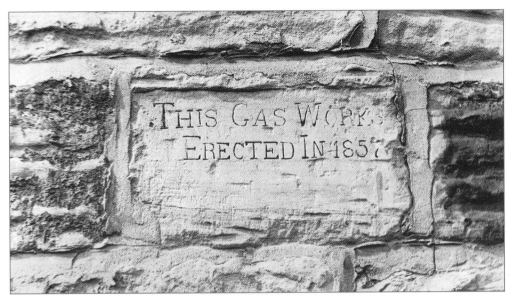

The original foundation stone at Elsecar Gas Works. (*Courtesy of Edwin Hugh Stenton and Amy Stenton*)

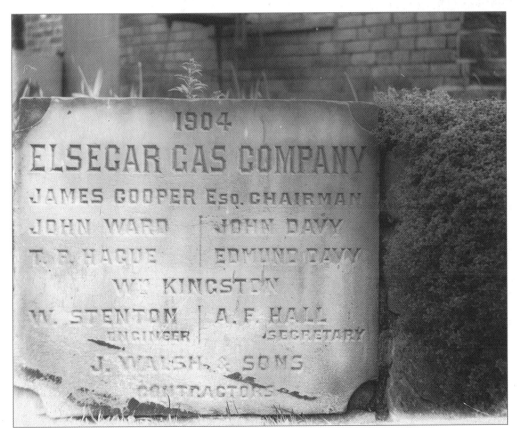

The foundation stone for the 1904 extension, with the inscribed names of the officials of the Elsecar Gas Company. (*Courtesy of Edwin Hugh Stenton and Amy Stenton*)

William Stenton (1860–1927), engineer and manager of Elsecar Gas Works. (*Courtesy of Edwin Hugh Stenton and Amy Stenton*)

Edwin Stenton, right, engineer and manager of Elsecar Gas Works, handing a retirement present to Frank Jones (1897–1965), 1964. (*Courtesy of Edwin Hugh Stenton and Amy Stenton*)

The Retort House, Elsecar Gas Works, 1926. (*Courtesy of Edwin Hugh Stenton and Amy Stenton*)

The extension of Elsecar Gas Works, showing no. 2 gas-holder completely empty, 1930s. The blacksmith's shop can be seen on the left and the original buildings of the gas works can be seen across Wath Road. (*Courtesy of Edwin Hugh Stenton and Amy Stenton*)

A full no. 2 ga
holder, 1930s.
(*Courtesy of
Edwin Hugh
Stenton and Am
Stenton*)

Billy Bowden and Walter Woodhead accepting a delivery of equipment for use at Elsecar Gas Works from th
Elsecar hauliers G. Dallinson & Son, 1920s. (*Courtesy of Edwin Hugh Stenton and Amy Stenton*)

The offices of Elsecar Gas Works, 1926, shortly after this building was erected. There was an adjacent weighbridge. This building forms part of the property purchased by Edwin Stenton in the 1960s. The building is currently occupied by C&G Engineering. (*Courtesy of Edwin Hugh Stenton and Amy Stenton*)

One of the by-products of coal gas production was coke. Here it is being loaded on to a railway wagon at the gas works, *c.* 1950. (*Courtesy of Edwin Hugh Stenton and Amy Stenton*)

PUBLIC NOTICE.

The Directors of the

ELSECAR GAS COMPANY

Have pleasure in Announcing that on and after
January 1st, 1885, their

PRICE FOR GAS

WILL BE

REDUCED

5d. per 1,000 Feet. Terms of Payment as heretofore.

They are also prepared to sell or let out on hire

STOVES

For Cooking & Heating Purposes

Which are Exceedingly Economical and very effective.

HINCHLIFFE & SON, PRINTERS, &c., HIGH STREET, ROTHERHAM.

An early advertisement for the Elsecar Gas Company. (*Courtesy of Edwin Hugh Stenton and Amy Stenton*)

Elsecar Gas Works, 1916. Standing in the back row, first left, is William Howse of 1 Wentworth Road, proprietor of the shop that once stood at the junction of Fitzwilliam Street and Wentworth Road, known as Howse's Corner. Standing next to him is Herbert Thickett, landlord of the Market Hotel. (*Courtesy of Edwin Hugh Stenton and Amy Stenton*)

Lady members of the Elsecar Cricket Club indulge in a game with the men, *c.* 1910. Just visible in the field behind, which is now the pitch and putt golf course in Elsecar Park, is what remained of the structure over the mineshaft, now covered by a concrete slab. (*Courtesy of Edwin Hugh Stenton and Amy Stenton*)

The New Yard (Elsecar Central Workshops) from the ruins of Elsecar ironworks, 1950s. (*Courtesy of Les Gaddass*)

The New Yard, looking towards Elsecar Canal basin, 1950s. In the centre foreground part of the ruins of Elsecar Ironworks can be seen. Elsecar Main Colliery can be seen on the skyline on the right. (*Courtesy of Les Gaddass*)

Elsecar Main Colliery from Wath Road, 1951. (*George Hardy collection*)

The footrill opened in 1723 to provide access to Low Wood Colliery and Elsecar Old Colliery. It was photographed on 7 February 1954 by George Hardy. The tunnel leading down to the workings was painted white; this was where Royalty was taken to view mine workings when they visited Earl Fitzwilliam's collieries at Elsecar. (*George Hardy collection*)

The Spez Bona opencast site was situated adjacent to Elsecar Reservoir on Fitzwilliam estate land once connected to Skiers Hall. This photograph looks towards the reservoir from Skiers Hall to Burying Lane footpath, February 1954. (*George Hardy collection*)

Spez Bona opencast site from Skiers Hall, 28 February 1954. (*George Hardy collection*)

Spez Bona opencast site showing old workings, 3 January 1954. The Barnsley bed seam of coal which can be seen by the entrance to the old mine workings is 9 ft 2 in thick, and outcrops close to the surface. Opencast scrapers revealed the coal stanchions, which had been left *in situ* to support the roof. During outcropping the machinery uncovered workings of the Skiers Spring drift mine, a mine worked using the pillar and post system of mining. Popularly known as Sludge Main, the drift was closed in the mid-1930s. During the lifetime of Skiers Spring drift mine very old mine workings were often uncovered, some over 200 years old. In an article which appeared in the *South Yorkshire Times* on 26 June 1954, one of the men who worked at Sludge Main recalled that roof-falls were frequent, and in places the roof was no more than a 4 ft thick seam of clay. (*George Hardy collection*)

Pumping shaft, Palmers Hill, Milton, February 1954. (*George Hardy collection*)

Hoyland and District Newsagents' Dance, held at Milton Hall, Elsecar, 9 March 1954. Standing, left to right: Margaret Rock, Trevor Rock, Les Dyson, Ernest Parkin, Mr Ferris, Reg Kenworthy. Middle row: Fay Bassindale, Dorothy Hague, Barbara Thornton, Christine Hague, Joyce Fletcher, Mary Parkin, Marjorie Dyson, Jean Ferris, Clarice Kenworthy. Front row: Mabel Shaw, Arthur Hague. (*Courtesy of Mabel Shaw and Sue Jenkins*)

Elsecar Church of England Junior School, 1955. Back row, left to right: Jacqueline Hall, Jean Hardy, -?-, Leslie Gaddass, Alan Micklethwaite, Alan Tasker, Andrew Hill, Philip Ackroyd, Susan Whittaker, Christine Howse. Middle row: Barbara Elden, Janet Smith, Christine Walker, Doreen Evans, Kathryn Hollingsworth, Angela Padgett, Wendy ?, Janet Dawson, Christine Brown, Susan Lockwood, Susan Drury. Front row: Geoffrey Cook, Brian Moore, Joan Camm, Marjorie Stenton, Linda Murray, Anne Bowler, Doreen Turner, Joyce Vaines, Vonnie Deaville, Stuart Sabin, Denis Thorpe. The schoolmistress is Mrs Lamb. (*Courtesy of Mrs Christine Walker*)

Elsecar Sunday School queen and attendants with the retiring queen and attendants at the crowning ceremony at the Milton Hall, Whit Sunday, 1958 or 1959. Back row, left to right: Susan Whittaker, Norma Pettinger, -?-, Christine Howse, Christine Walker. Front row: Margaret Bamforth, Jean Taylor, Andrea Green (retiring queen), Sheila Lomas (queen), Rita Bamforth, Gillian Whittlestone, Richard O'Brien. The Sunday School queen and entourage headed the procession during the Whit Monday Walk, a popular event in Elsecar village life. It was a joint venture between the combined churches, namely Holy Trinity, Elsecar Wesleyan Reform, Elsecar Congregational and St John's (off Wath Road and now a private house). (*Courtesy of Mrs Christine Walker*)

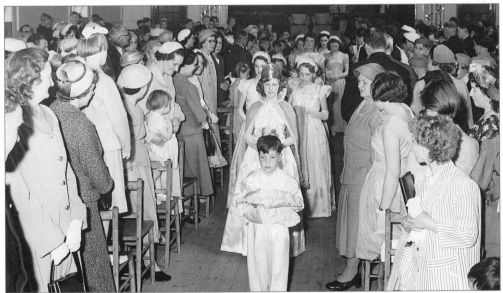

Pageboy Richard O'Brien leads the newly crowned combined churches Sunday School queen and her entourage out of Milton Hall. (*Courtesy of Mrs Christine Walker*)

A Christmas party at Elsecar Wesleyan Reform Sunday School, 1962. Back row, left to right: Mrs Walsh, Mrs Gillott, Jean Walsh, Kathleen Marples. Fourth row: Ian Jowett, Jeanette Gaddass, Lorraine Nicholls, the O'Brien twins, Gerald and Ronald, Philip Harling. Third row: Amanda Deaville, Karen Johnson, Kevin Johnson, Gillian Leech, Michael Gilberthorpe, Christine Nicholls. Second row: Anne Foster, Geoffrey Howse, -?-, Anne Gaddass, Peter O'Brien. Front row: Paul Bostwick, Howard Gaddass. (*Doreen Howse collection*)

Kenneth Masheder on the exhibition stand of the Milton Motor Co. at Hoyland Trade Fair, Milton Hall, October 1968. Masheder's held the Daf franchise until 1972. (*Joan Masheder collection*)

Earl Fitzwilliam's private railway station (opened in 1870 by the 6th Earl), which after restoration in the 1990s now forms part of Elsecar Heritage Centre. (*George Hardy collection*)

The Old Row, 3 July 1997. In external appearance very little has changed since the row of cottages was built in the 1790s. (*George Hardy collection*)

5

Wentworth

The Mausoleum, showing the interior of the ground-floor chamber, with the statue of Charles, 2nd Marquess of Rockingham by Joseph Nollekens. (*George Hardy collection*)

Main Street, Wentworth, *c.* 1900. This street, once known as 'The Town Street', was tarmacadamised in 1914. On the left is part of the complex of buildings belonging to the George and Dragon Hotel, and on the right is Pole's shop, which was Wentworth's principal shop for over a hundred years until the Barnsley British Co-operative Society bought the business in 1916. They traded in Pole's former premises until February 1974, after which the building stood empty. Fortunately the Wentworth newsagents decided to expand and moved into Pole's former shop. It is currently known as the Village Stores. (*Sandra Hague collection*)

The George and Dragon Hotel, when John Rimes was 'mine host', early 1900s. Formerly one of Wentworth village's grander homes, the building dates from at least the seventeenth century, and during the early eighteenth century it was being used as an inn. The Pepper family was closely associated with this popular hostelry during the eighteenth and nineteenth centuries. It is generally believed that the part of the building to the right of the photograph, known as the 'Court House', may once have been where the manorial courts were held. From the time of the 5th Earl Fitzwilliam until the latter part of the lifetime of the 10th Earl, the George and Dragon remained closed on Sundays. (*Sandra Hague collection*)

Paradise Square, Wentworth, *c.* 1910. Known by this name from about 1900, the buildings seen here were once a farm. The farmhouse is at the top left of the photograph, although the original farmhouse is believed to have been part of one of the adjacent buildings. This attractive group was converted into cottages during the eighteenth century. (*Sandra Hague collection*)

Street Cottages from Street Lane, April 1994. Hoober Stand is on the horizon. (*George Hardy collection*)

Wentworth School and the almshouses, *c.* 1900. The school and almshouses were formerly known as the Poor Hospital and were situated between Wentworth and Harley. 'His Honour Wentworth' was responsible for these buildings in 1716, after he established 'a perpetual fund for clothing, teaching and instructing in reading, writing and casting up of accounts, fifty poor children, boys and girls in the Charity School at Barrow in the Chapelry of Wentworth'. The school was in the part of the building seen here, the single-storey buildings behind serving as almshouses. By the 1830s the school had become overcrowded and in 1835 the 5th Earl Fitzwilliam built a new school to accommodate the girls. Boys and girls were taught in these two establishments until 1943, when educational reforms enabled the Wentworth schools to teach boys and girls between the ages of five and eleven. Older children went outside the village to continue their education at secondary level. (*Sandra Hague collection*)

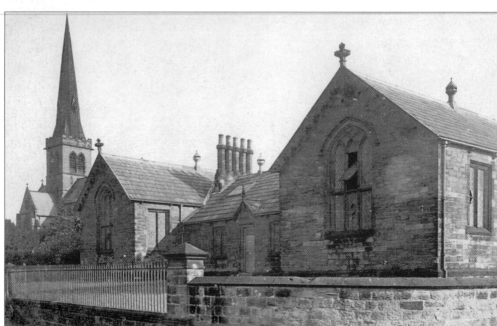

Wentworth Girls' School, *c.* 1900. (*George Hardy collection*)

oly Trinity Church, Wentworth, from Church Field Lane,
950s. (*George Hardy collection*)

n interior view of the Wentworth chapel, Holy Trinity Church, showing the altar tomb of the grandparents of
1e 1st Earl of Strafford. (*George Hardy collection*)

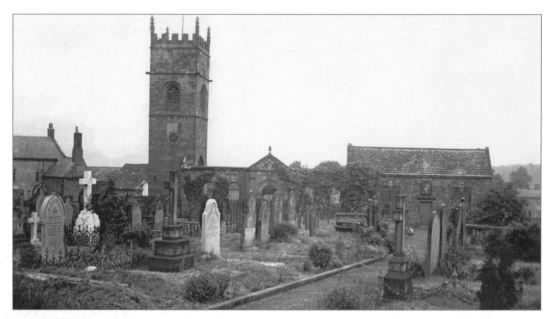

Wentworth Old Church as it appeared in about 1900, over twenty years after it had been partly dismantle (*George Hardy collection*)

Today the church is ruined except for the tower, chancel and Wentworth chapel, which comprises the sou chapel, containing the chancel and north chapel (known as the Wentworth chapel), of the medieval churc Wentworth was originally part of the enormous parish of Wath-upon-Dearne. Holy Trinity Church was built as chapel of ease in the late twelfth or early thirteenth century on land donated by the Wentworth family; the p was large enough to provide a burial ground. Part of the church was built in the Decorated style, widely used the fourteenth century. Repairs to the structure and some rebuilding work were required by 1491. On 18 Augu that year a commission was issued by the ecclesiastical court in York to William, Bishop of Dromore, 'consecrate anew the Chapel of Wentworth, with the chapelyard in the parish of Wath-upon-Dearne'. Followi the 1534 Act of Supremacy and the Dissolution of the Monasteries, which followed, Monk Bretton Priory w dissolved in 1538, and towards the end of the sixteenth century several of its Norman features, including pilla and other stonework, were incorporated in the structure of Holy Trinity Church. This has made the precise dati of the church difficult for architectural historians, but these additions clearly pre-date any of the identifiab original features which survive today. This architectural salvage material from Monk Bretton Priory w purchased by Thomas Wentworth (1478–1548), great-great-grandfather of the 1st Earl of Strafford, shortly aft the Reformation, and left to the church in his will, which had been drawn up in 1646. He left to the chapel Wentworth for the building of an aisle: 'All the pillars with the imbondings and all other stone they shall need have, which I bought off the King's visitors at Burton Grange'. He also left specific instructions to be buried clo to his ancestors in the church at Wentworth. His wishes were carried out and his brass is in the north aisle.

His eldest son William died the following year. William's son Thomas and his wife Margaret lie beneath impressive altar tomb, topped by intricately carved, recumbent, alabaster effigies. Close by is part of a double alt tomb belonging to the Gascoigne family dating from *c.* 1450, with a recumbent male in armour and a (now bac damaged) female effigy carved in alabaster. This monument was rescued from the ruins of Monk Bretton Prio and brought to Wentworth. An exact identification of which of the Gascoignes this tomb commemorates has yet be made. It is thought that this monument was brought to Wentworth because Thomas Wentworth's w Margaret was a Gascoigne heiress (who brought the Gawthorpe estate into the Wentworth family's ownershi and the tomb belongs to direct members of her family.

Other monuments include hanging wall monuments to Sir William Wentworth (died 1614), his wife Ann (di 1611) and their son Thomas, the 1st (though he is more often referred to as the Great) Earl of Strafford. This sty of monument was a relatively new feature and came into fashion towards the end of the sixteenth century.

...e monument to Lord Strafford's parents seen here is a ...e example of its type, and has been attributed to the ...mish sculptor Nicholas Johnson. It shows Sir William ...d Lady Wentworth kneeling at a *prie-dieu* (prayer desk). ... William is wearing armour, and he and his wife are ...picted in a Renaissance-inspired setting. Below them, in ...e part of the monument known as the predella, there are ...rved figures of their children. Their eldest son, the future ...rl of Strafford, is depicted much larger than his siblings. ...e Earl of Strafford's own wall monument is situated next ...it. (*George Hardy collection*)

The monument to Thomas Wentworth, 1st Earl of Strafford, *c.* 1900. It was erected by his son William, 2nd Earl of Strafford. The inscription reads:

THOMAS WENTWORTH
Earl of Strafford, Viscount Wentworth, Baron Wentworth of Wentworth Woodhouse, Newmarch, Oversley and Raby, Lord Lieutenant of Ireland, Lord President of the North of England; and Knight of the most noble Order of the Garter. His birth was upon Good Friday the 13th Ap. 1593. His death Upon the 12th May 1641. His soule through the Mercy Of God lives in eternal blisse and his memory will Never dye in these kingdoms.

(*Sandra Hague collection*)

The fine wall monument to the 2nd Earl of Strafford. (*George Hardy collection*)

Lord Strafford actually lies buried in York Minster, with his nephew and heir Thomas Watson-Wentworth and the 1st and 2nd Marquesses of Rockingham. The hatchments of the two marquesses can be seen high up on the walls. Beneath the wall monument is the Gascoigne monument and on the right is the altar tomb of the grandparents of the 1st Earl of Strafford. There are also floor monuments, some now unrecognisable, to other members of the house of Wentworth, a monument to the Great Earl of Strafford's steward Richard Marris (1635), and to members of the Rokeby and Skiers families. An interesting and unusual monument near the vestry door is believed to date from the fourteenth century. It is one of the rarest examples of the type of monument that depicts the rank or profession of the deceased: a crudely carved slab, known locally as the 'archer's grave', it has a cross and a bow carved into it. Steps lead from the vestry down to a corridor leading into the Fitzwilliam vault, built in 1827 to contain members of the Wentworth-Fitzwilliam family. The size of the vault can be seen from outside the church.

Holy Trinity Church as it has appeared since 1962, when the top of the tower was ripped off during a storm. In the churchyard an ashlar plinth and vault cover, consisting of two chamfered stone slabs weighing 40 tons each, covers the vault. Rectangular in shape, this massive vault cover is surrounded by iron railings, set between ten iron piers with lozenge shaped panels. There are fleur-de-lis finials to the lower and upper rails. (*George Hardy collection*)

The chancel, Wentworth Old Church, early 1900s. The monument to the 1st Earl of Strafford can just be seen in the top right foreground. Below Strafford's monument is the communion rail. Having served other Wentworth residents, the bier on the right of the photograph in the Wentworth chapel was used to transport the coffin of the 8th Earl Fitzwilliam from Wentworth Woodhouse to the New Church for his funeral service in May 1948. He was buried in a grave adjacent to his parents in the family's private burial ground. (*Sandra Hague collection*)

Around a panel at the top of the railings of the Fitzwilliam vault an inscription reads: 'This place of burial was constructed A.D. MDCCCXXIV By William Earl Fitzwilliam and Charles William Viscount Milton for the Wentworth Branch of their descendants in the hope that they may pass through things temporal, that they may lose not the things eternal.' Fewer than a quarter of the thirty available spaces are occupied, as Countess Harriet, wife of the 6th Earl Fitzwilliam, herself a staunch Scots Presbyterian, considered the vault too ostentatious, and had a private burial ground laid out on the south side of the New Church. She and her husband are buried there, as are the 7th Earl and Countess, the 8th Earl and Countess, the 9th Earl and other family members. Other Fitzwilliams, including the 10th Earl and Countess, are buried at Marholm, near Peterborough, on the Fitzwilliam ancestral estate surrounding Milton Hall.

The Fitzwilliam private burial ground, which is to the south of the New Church. The photograph shows the double grave of the 7th Earl and Countess Fitzwilliam, and to the right of it the grave of the 8th Earl and Countess Fitzwilliam. (*George Hardy collection*)

In 1684 the 2nd Earl of Strafford spent £700 on the church in memory of his wife, the former Lady Henrietta Maria Stanley (daughter of the Earl of Derby), whose initials can be seen both in the windows and in the woodwork. During this phase of building the nave was remodelled. According to the distinguished architectural historian Sir Nikolaus Pevsner, the external appearance of the parallel east gables suggests that they date from the early seventeenth century. If this is true then the work might have been carried out on the instructions of either the 1st Earl of Strafford's father or grandfather, during or after the phase of building which incorporated parts of Monk Bretton Priory into the fabric of the church. By the middle of the nineteenth century Holy Trinity Church, Wentworth, was once again in need of extensive repair. The 6th Earl Fitzwilliam and his family decided against this, opting instead to build a new church as a fitting memorial to the 5th Earl and Countess Fitzwilliam. Several designs were considered before one by J.L. Pearson, in the Gothic Revival Style, was chosen in 1872.

The last Sunday service in the old church was on 29 July 1877. On Tuesday 31 July the New Church was consecrated by the Archbishop of York. Shortly afterwards the nave and north aisle of the Old Church were demolished, leaving the south wall, tower, chancel, lady chapel (also known as the north or Wentworth chapel) and vestry intact. Since that time services have been held in the New Church. The Old Church was thereafter used as a mortuary chapel. In 1925 the 7th Earl Fitzwilliam restored the chancel and Wentworth chapel. Electricity and central heating followed. As the private chapel in Wentworth Woodhouse was in the part of the mansion being used by Lady Mabel College, on the death of Countess Maud in 1967 her coffin was laid in state in the Old Church, prior to her funeral service in the New Church and her subsequent burial in the Fitzwilliams' private burial ground beside her husband, the 7th Earl. The Old Church was declared redundant in 1974 and taken over by the Redundant Churches Fund (now the Churches Conservation Trust). What remains of the Old Church has been restored in recent years.

The New Church, Wentworth. Like the Old Church, this too was dedicated to the Holy Trinity. For an interior view see page 102 of *Around Hoyland*. (*George Hardy collection*)

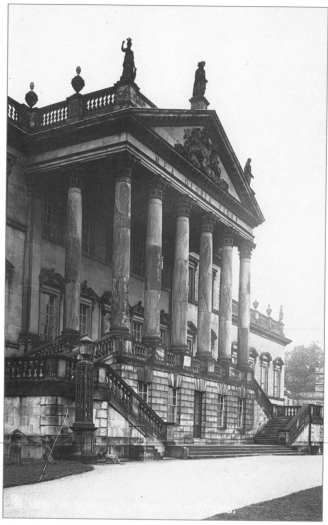

The central portion of Wentworth Woodhouse, showing the steps leading to the portico, *c.* 1900. At this time William Thomas Spencer Wentworth-Fitzwilliam, 6th Earl Fitzwilliam KG, was living here. He died on 20 February 1902, having been earl since 1857. Lord Fitzwilliam appears in a recent study by the *Sunday Times* of the wealthiest 200 people in Britain since 1066 to the year 2000 (monarchs are excluded). The 6th Earl's wealth was calculated in terms of its worth in 2000, this being £3.3 billion, making him equal 125th wealthiest, a position he shares with his ancestor, Charles, 2nd Marquess of Rockingham. It also makes the 6th Earl Fitzwilliam the third wealthiest person to have lived in Great Britain in the twentieth century. Another famous resident of Wentworth Woodhouse also makes this list. When the axe fell, severing the head of Thomas Wentworth, Earl of Strafford, from his body, on 12 May 1641, he was worth £6.1 billion, making him equal 61st on the wealthy list. William de Warene (died 1088), of Conisborough Castle, who owned extensive lands in and around Hoyland, is at position number one. In today's money he would be worth £57.6 billion. It is also interesting to look at costs of the building work carried out at Wentworth Woodhouse during the eighteenth and early nineteenth centuries. Based on the known costs of building work calculated in today's prices, the cost of undertaking a similar project at the beginning of the twenty-first century would exceed £550 million. (*Sandra Hague collection*)

The East Front of Wentworth Woodhouse, *c.* 1900. The Scotch bullocks and buffaloes were once a popular sight in Wentworth Park. (*George Hardy collection*)

The Fitzwilliam state landau. James Morgan, coachman, is holding the reins. (*George Hardy collection*)

The Octagon Lodge, Wentworth, *c.* 1900. This is one of many eighteenth-century lodges which are scattered around the estate. It is situated at the gates of Wentworth Park, opposite the end of Clayfields Lane. It has stood sentinel to the principal carriageway to Wentworth Woodhouse for over two centuries. (*Sandra Hague collection*)

Members of the Wentworth-Fitzwilliam family and their guests gather outside the East Front of Wentworth Woodhouse, on the occasion of the christening of the 7th Earl Fitzwilliam's heir Viscount Milton, 11 February 1911. (*Sandra Hague collection*)

Roasting an ox in the grounds of Wentworth Woodhouse, 11 February 1911. This formed part of the celebrations marking the christening of Viscount Milton. (*George Hardy collection*)

Viscount Milton and his sister Lady Helena Wentworth-Fitzwilliam, at the garden party held for soldiers' comforts, 22 August 1918. (*Sandra Hague collection*)

Viscount Milton and Lady Helena at the Garden Party held for Soldiers' Comforts Aug 22. 1918.

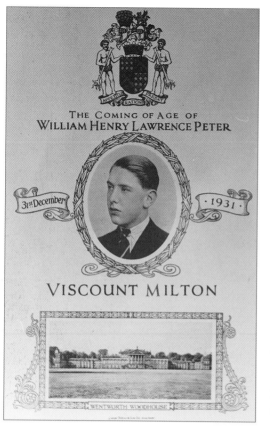

William Henry Lawrence Peter Wentworth-Fitzwilliam, b
Viscount Milton on New Year's Eve, 31 December 1910.
He was son of William Charles de Meuron, 7th Earl
Fitzwilliam, and Countess Fitzwilliam, the former Lady
Maude Frederica Elizabeth Dundas, daughter of the
Marquess of Zetland. Lord and Lady Fitzwilliam had five
children. Viscount Milton, known as Peter by his family,
affectionately known as the 'Lordy' by almost everyone e
locally, was their youngest child and only son. His sisters
were the Ladies Donatia, Elfrida, Joan and Helena. Lord
Milton enjoyed playing cricket, and the Viscount Milton :
played matches locally, some within Wentworth Park on
lawn immediately outside the East Front of Wentworth
Woodhouse. The Lordy was educated at Eton, and marri
Olive Dorothea Plunkett, daughter of the Hon. and most
Rev. Benjamin J. Plunkett, former Bishop of Meath, at the
St Patrick's Church of Ireland Cathedral in Dublin on
19 April 1933. A ship chartered by Lord Fitzwilliam took
over a hundred estate employees to Dublin to see the Lor
married. There was to be only one child from the marria
a daughter, Lady Juliet, was born in 1935. Viscount Milt
became the 8th Earl on the death of his father, on
15 February 1943. This commemorative gold embossed
card was produced for his twenty-first birthday celebratic
and was given to Isadore and Clara Susannah Howse by
7th Earl and Countess Fitzwilliam. Peter Wentworth-
Fitzwilliam, 8th Earl Fitzwilliam, was killed in a plane cra
on 13 May 1948. (*Author's collection*)

A celebration bonfire at Hoober Stand, 31 December 1931, to mark the coming of age of Viscount Milton. (*George Hardy collection*)

The statue within the Ionic Temple at the southern end of the Great South Terrace, Wentworth Woodhouse, *c*. 1910. (*Sandra Hague collection*)

This view of the Roundhouse (also known as Saxon Tower) from Clayfields Lane was taken in September 1995. (*George Hardy collection*)

The residents of Wentworth Woodhouse had indulged in hunting in one form or another for centuries. The 2r Marquess of Rockingham owned a fine pack of stag hounds: some particular favourites from this pack we painted by George Stubbs. During the latter part of the eighteenth century fox hunting took over from sta hunting as the preferred sport on Earl Fitzwilliam's Wentworth Estates. When William, 4th Earl Fitzwilliar inherited his uncle's estates he brought with him a tradition of fox hunting, which had been taking place on h ancestral estate surrounding Milton Hall, near Peterborough, since before 1760, and on his family's Irish estate for a considerable time before. By the beginning of the twentieth century no name was more closely associate with fox hunting than that of Fitzwilliam. The Fitzwilliam Foxhounds covered country in Northamptonshire an Huntingdonshire that was nearly 30 miles long by nearly 20 miles wide. It may be that hounds were brougl from Milton to hunt the Wentworth country at first. By 1860 Earl Fitzwilliam's (Wentworth) Foxhounds we hunting country about 20 miles at its greatest width east to west and 15 miles north to south. At its norther boundary it adjoined the Badsworth, on the west boundary the country was not hunted, on the south it adjoine the Barlow and on the east Earl Fitzwilliam's (Grove). Earl Fitzwilliam's (Wentworth) Foxhounds were kept in th complex of buildings known as The Kennels, in the village, near the Roundhouse. This photograph shows Ea Fitzwilliam's (Wentworth) Foxhounds in Wentworth Park during the early twentieth century. On the right George A. Wilson, Master of Hounds. He owned racing stables and lived at Butterthwaite, Barnsley Roa Ecclesfield. (*Cyril Slinn collection*)

1907 the 7th Earl took over Viscount Galway's (Grove) Foxhounds and renamed them Earl Fitzwilliam's (Grove)
xhounds. They hunted country extending 24 miles north to south and 30 miles east to west in
ottinghamshire, Yorkshire and Derbyshire. The kennels were originally at Grove but from 1887 were at Serlby.
unting continued until 1929 when increasing industrialisation had reduced the country for both Earl
zwilliam's (Wentworth) Foxhounds and (Grove) Foxhounds to such an extent that the 7th Earl decided to call it
day, and hunting with both packs came to an end. Although the Fitzwilliam Hunt is still an important feature of
untry life at Milton, on the Fitzwilliam (Wentworth) Estates, the Yorkshire estates are seldom hunted today.
nce the disappearance of much of the heavy industry in South Yorkshire the country has improved, and in
cent years the Badsworth has occasionally hunted country where Earl Fitzwilliam's (Wentworth) Foxhounds
ce held sway. This photograph shows Earl Fitzwilliam's (Grove) Foxhounds in Bawtry Market Place on 15 March
09. Major G.H. Peake of Bawtry Hall, with moustache and silk top hat, is mounted on his horse to the right of
e picture. (*Author's collection*)

The Rockingham Arms, the largest of Wentworth's two remaining public houses. Although there is a datestone the stables of 1814, the main part of the complex of buildings is considerably older, and probably dates from least as early as the middle of the eighteenth century. (*George Hardy collection*)

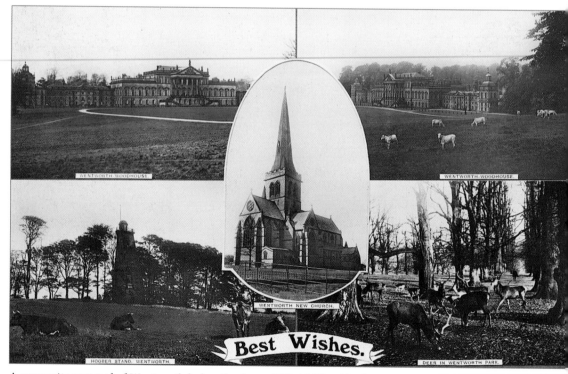

A composite postcard of Wentworth before the Second World War. (*Sandra Hague collection*)

6

Jump

The Flying Dutchman during the second half of the nineteenth century. (*Keith Hopkinson collection*)

Jump Hall Farm, early twentieth century. (*Keith Hopkinson collection*)

When asked 'Where do you come from?' many Jumpers have been faced with shrieks of laughter when they ha
replied 'Jump'. This laughter stems from surprise at this most unusual of place names. Imagine the astonishme
of strangers, travelling along the B6096, being confronted by the road sign 'Jump 1 mile'. There are several stor
about its origin. Local legend maintains that the name derives from the people who had to jump across the dyke
the valley which lies between Hoyland and Jump. Another legend is that before the village streets were laid out t
foundations for various properties had already been dug, and the builders had to jump between plots. Both the
theories are not without foundation, as the Danish word *gump* and the Swedish word *gumpa* both mean to cr
over by leaping, and the area was invaded by both Swedish and Danish marauders. However, as Jump Far
existed at least 300 years before the village was even thought of that theory does not hold. Another theory has
origins in hunting. As the land from Hoyland falls sharply into the valley, men on horseback chased their quar
to the spot where the land levelled, but if the quarry crossed the valley the riders had to jump or fall. Or one ma
turn to Mr Armitage Goodall's *Place Names of South West Yorkshire* for the solution to the name's origin. He class
together the three names Jum, Jumble and Jump, and goes on to quote from Wright's *English Dialect Dictionar*
which states that 'Jumble Hole' is a rough, bushy, uncultivated hollow. Who can say this is not a likely contend
for Jump Hole, which could be shortened to Jump? Another interesting fact came to light recently, thanks to Mi
Sandra Hague. Newman and Bond, solicitors, of 35 Church Street, Barnsley, released several documents th
related to her family, the firm's oldest clients. Sandra's great-great-great-great-grandfather, William Hague, wh
died in 1810, purchased 3 acres and 3 perches of land, known as Round Hill Close, in the township of Wombwe
from Anthony St Leger Esquire, of Park Hill, Firbeck, on 11 September 1777. This was none other tha
Lieutenant-Colonel (later Major General) Anthony St Leger, distinguished soldier, Member of Parliament, one-tin
Governor of St Lucia, landowner, sportsman, and friend of Charles, 2nd Marquess of Rockingham. St Leger, aft
whom the oldest classic turf race in the world was named, at the suggestion of Lord Rockingham, was a
enthusiastic follower of the turf. He had purchased the land in 1774. Could his purchase of this land have ha
anything to do with the breeding of horses for racing or hunting? Had there been a stud farm on the site, o
nearby, or a practice racetrack in Jump like the one owned by Lord Rockingham in Swinton? In reality it was no
unusual for landowners to make purchases such as this to exploit mineral resources but it is just possible that th
name does relate in some way to horse breeding, the horses being required to jump across the dyke to Hoyland.

The obvious conclusion to be drawn is that the village simply took its name from the farm, and that all th
theories relate to the name of the farm – and not to the village at all.

ımp School, 1900. (*Courtesy of Mabel Shaw and Sue Jenkins*)

Vhatever its actual origins, the name used for Jump village is not that old, compared with others in the locality. Before 1800 the village of Jump did not exist, the land which it later occupied being known as Hemingfield Common. However, Jump Hole Farm (which later became Jump Hall Farm) is mentioned in the Wentworth Manor Court Rolls of 1576. Thomas Lodge, who lived at Jump Hall Farm as a boy during the early twentieth century, told Peter Marsh that he remembered a date of 1510 over a lintel in an old part of the house. The farm was situated just within Hoyland township. In 1605 Richard Townend of Blacker bequeathed to Robert Swinden two fields lying in the enclosed area known as High Fields, in the township of Wombwell; at the time they were being used by John Hill, who lived at Jump or Jump Hole Farm. In 1623 John Hill of Nether Hoyland bequeathed to his son John the lands in Wombwell known as Wiskett Royds. Over a hundred years later Wiskett Royds still remained part of Jump Farm. In 1723 another John Hill sold to his son Thomas Jump Farm, and also some land close to Bark Farm, now known as Bark House, situated in Hoyland's Market Street. In 1749 Thomas Hill and Sir William Wentworth Bt of Bretton Hall, signed an indenture concerning Jump Farm and other lands within South Yorkshire. A gravestone in Wentworth churchyard reads: 'Thomas Hill of Jump, Gent, died 6 November 1755'. In 1771 William Shaw owned Jump Farm, and in 1842, when William Vizard wanted to make a railway incline from Hoyland Silkstone Colliery to Elsecar Canal basin, he bought land belonging to Jump Farm from another William Shaw, of Great Houghton. The last tenant of Jump Hall Farm was Bernard Hazelwood, who rented it from the trustees of the late Richard Wadsworth, one-time landlord of the Rockingham Arms, Wentworth. Jump Hall Farm was taken off the Hoyland rating list in 1954 and was demolished soon afterwards. Lilac Crescent was built on the site of the farm and its outbuildings.

A composite view of Jump and district, early 1900s. Featured in the centre is St George's Church. Hemingfield Road, Wombwell Wood and Wombwell railway station are also featured. (*Keith Hopkinson collection*)

The village of Jump grew up a short distance from Jump Hall Farm, within the township of Wombwell. Joseph Dickenson's map of 1750 shows Jump Farm and describes it simply as Jump. On Dickenson's map the site of the present village is described as 'Hemingfield Common now enclosed'. Jeffrey's map, also of 1771, shows the site of the village as being uninhabited.

Mining had been taking place in Jump Valley since the middle of the eighteenth century. These were drifts into the valley sides or shallow mines, which worked coal that outcropped close to the surface. A few families settled in Jump Valley during the following years. William, 4th Earl Fitzwilliam, opened his Jump Colliery which worked the Barnsley bed seam on 14 September 1816. The expansion of that mine in the years that followed, and the opening of other mines in the vicinity, gradually led to the development of more housing throughout the area.

In 1830 the village of Jump still did not exist, and the township of Wombwell amounted to 836 inhabitants. By 1850 the population of Wombwell had doubled; in 1861 it had reached 3,344, and the village of Jump accounted for 1,000 souls, almost a third of the township's population. From this it is clear that once building had begun in the new village Jump's expansion was rapid. In 1841 housing had been built from the present Wentworth Road halfway along the lower side of the present Church Street. In 1849 some houses appear on the Ordnance Survey map down Kit Royd and in the part of the village lying near Greenside Lane. Public houses were also built, and in the 1861 census the Flying Dutchman, the Duke of Cambridge, the Wellington and the Red White and Blue appear. From about 1850 the Dawes family, who ran both Elsecar and Milton Ironworks, were responsible for the rapid development of housing and other facilities in Jump. The family's influence extended over a thirty-year period. They owned ironworks in Staffordshire, and brought workers from that area to work in their ironworks in Elsecar and Milton. They built houses in Hoyland, known as Sebastopol, and in Jump built Milton Square (a series of terraces), which became known as Turkey. The Wentworth Road area of Jump became known as Inkerman. These names stem from the Crimean War (1854–6). Although Earl Fitzwilliam's Jump Colliery closed on 30 September 1858, work was available elsewhere, including the collieries at Hemingfield and Tingle Bridge. Miners, ironworkers and various supporting tradesmen and their families began to fill the newly built properties. Places of worship and a school were soon required. A Wesleyan Reform Chapel was built in 1855, and a Church of England schoolroom followed, built chiefly at the expense of George Dawes. He also contributed to the building of St George's Church, erected in the centre of the village in Church Street, and opened for worship in 1880. A new Wesleyan Reform Chapel was built in the same year, the old chapel being used as a Sunday school. No doubt the closure of both the Elsecar and Milton Ironworks on 30 January 1884 caused some anxiety in Jump, but its growth as a village continued. In 1891 the Barnsley British Co-operative Society opened a store there. By the end of the century Jump had been well and truly established on the map.

ady supporters of Jump Home Guard Football Team, during the Second World War. Back row, left to right: little
irl on extreme left, -?-, Eva Turnton, Mrs Williams, Dolly Hopkinson, Annie Peake (Ball), Lena Travers, Rene
ackleton and Evelyn Chapman. Front row: Alice Fellowes, Mrs Roby, Florence Peake, Mrs Cissie Jackson.
Courtesy of Rose Willis)

y 1901 the name Jump was causing embarrassment to some of its residents, who had the idea of changing the
ame to Woodlands. The majority of Jumpers were outraged by this and gave the idea a resounding no, so the
ame remains. However, the proposed name change was preserved in a stone over some shops in Church Street,
vhich bears the inscription 'Woodlands Market Place 1903'. Perhaps the idea of changing the name stemmed
·om some residents wishing to give a gentler name to their village, in an attempt to shed the reputation Jump had
ained for being a rough area in the early twentieth century. Policemen went on the beat in pairs when patrolling
he rows of terraced houses known as Turkey. Those houses, and many of Jump's original properties, disappeared
nder a slum clearance programme. The site of Turkey is now occupied by semi-detached houses, flats, and old
eople's bungalows.

Over the years Jump has been home to many colourful characters, who to outsiders may well have given the
ppearance of being less than genteel – but many of the so-called rougher elements gave Jump a distinctive
haracter. It developed a unique village atmosphere and a healthy community spirit existed. Some of the village's
lder residents have fond memories of old Jump, and regret the demolition of the heart of the original village.

Jump children, *c*. 1963. Featured in the photograph are Philip Baker, Colin Bailey, Eric Hopkinson, Kevin Hough, Christine Bailey, Anne Lockwood, Sarah Mott, Carol Jackson, Terry Wroe, Alan Fearon, Susan Booth, Margaret Jubb, Sandra Dickson, Ian Adams, Stuart Hopkinson, Carol and Kevin Carnell, Ian Wroe, Hazel Hopkinson, Steven Hopkinson, Mary Booth, Wendy Booth, Colin Jennings, Jane Jennings, Josephine Booth and Pauline Hislop. (*Courtesy of Sarah Mott*)

More Jump children, *c*. 1963. Some well-known Jump families are represented, among a few unknown faces. Seated on the wall, left to right: Martin Edgar, -?-, Janet Brookes, Linda Cash, Joan Stafford. The children both standing and seated include Alan Hawksworth, Liz Golby, Hazel Hopkinson, Joyce Crane, Linda Cooper, Roberta Eckleton, Terry Wroe, Sarah Mott, Susan Fellows, Wendy Peake, M. Peake, Susan Greavson, Janet North, Stephen Clegg, Stuart Hopkinson, Philip Baker and Clary Hackleton. (*Courtesy of Sarah Mott*)

7

The Surrounding Area

Park Well House, Rockley, early 1900s. (*Courtesy of Chris Thawley*)

Brick making began at Skiers Spring Brickworks in the summer of 1877. One of the original partners wa James Smith, and although the works were taken over by Earl Fitzwilliam, they were known by many locally a Smith's Brickworks. The brickworks were situated on a piece of level ground, close to the single-track railwa line near the junction of Stead Lane and Broadcarr Road. The raw materials to make the bricks were readi available locally. There was a clay pit a short distance away, to the south of the brickworks, and neighbourin shale tips, legacies from ironstone mines, which had been worked until shortly before the brickworks opene The clay pit served a double purpose, because a 30 inch seam of coal, known as Kent's thick coal, outcroppe at this point, which provided fuel for firing the brick-kilns. Both clay and coal were transported from the cla pit by means of a short, narrow tramway, which ran under the Midland Railway line, after it was constructe in 1897. James Smith and his partner Mr Hitchmough were later joined by a Mr Pitt, but the brickworks wa eventually taken over by Earl Fitzwilliam, with Mr Smith's son as manager. During its most productive perio 10,000 bricks were being made each day. Skiers Spring Brickworks closed in 1919. This photograph was take in 1898. (*Jack Howse collection*)

Skiers Spring Wood (more usually referred to as the Spring Wood) and Broadcarr Road, winter 1970. (*Joan Masheder collection*)

Coming off the roundabout at Birdwell at junction 36 of the M1 motorway, 1970. The pit tip of Rockingham Colliery can be seen in the background. On the skyline on the right is Rockingham Miners' Welfare Hall. (*Joan Masheder collection*)

An aerial view of Rainborough Grange, in Brampton Bierlow, close to its border with Hoyland township, *c.* 195(

In the time of Edward the Confessor Alric, a Saxon lord, was in possession of the manor of Cawthorne. After 106
the lands were given to Ilbert de Lacy, but Alric remained as tenant. Alric was succeeded by his son Swaine, wh
died in 1130. Swaine was in turn succeeded by Adam Fitzswain. In 1090 Robert de Lacy, a son of Ilbert de Lac
founded the Priory of St John of Pontefract. Swaine had given the church of Silkstone and the chapel (
Cawthorne, with certain lands, towards its foundation. Adam Fitzswain wished to endow a monastery of his ow
foundation, and to that end granted the Prior of Pontefract 'the site of the monastery to be called of the Blesse
Mary Magdalene of Lund, with Bretton and Newhall and Rainesborough (Rainborough) and Linthwaite an
whatever be held in Brampton and between Dearne and Staincliff as far as Meresbrook, together with the mills
Dearne and Lund etc.' All that remains of Monk Bretton Priory, founded by Adam Fitzswain in 1153, is situated (
the east of what is now the borough of Barnsley, at Cundy Cross. Originally of the Cluniac order, both priorie
were subservient to the Abbot of Cluny, the head of the order. From its foundation Monk Bretton Priory had bee
made dependent on Pontefract. Never a comfortable relationship, friction arose between the two priories, which i
1279 culminated in an act of contumacy, resulting in the monks of Bretton being excommunicated. In 1281 th
monks changed their allegiance to the Benedictine order, and they remained faithful to that order until Mon
Bretton Priory was dissolved by Henry VIII in 1538.

The monks established granges on the land given by Adam Fitzswain. This may have involved adapting existin
buildings, as was clearly the case at Rainborough (because a building of substantial size stood on this land befor
Domesday Book), or building an entirely new grange. (A grange is simply a country house with farm building
attached.) After the Dissolution of the Monasteries the numerous estates belonging to Monk Bretton Priory passe
to new owners. The Rainborough Grange estate eventually came under the ownership of the Wentworth famil
from nearby Wentworth Woodhouse, and remained in their ownership until Rainborough Grange and part of th
former Rainborough Grange Estate were sold to the National Coal Board in the 1960s.

As for Rainborough Grange itself, its existence is a mystery to the vast majority of local people. Very few ar
even aware that it was an important feature on the local landscape for over 900 years. The first Rainboroug
Grange was built at the head of a field known as the Starbank, situated close to Rainborough Park, from ston
quarried on its own estate. The Rainborough Grange which replaced it, seen here, was built further down the hi
and probably dates from the sixteenth or early seventeenth century. It was built about 25 yd from the quarry
which provided the stone to construct all the buildings on the estate. Rainborough Grange can be seen in th
middle of the photograph, on the extreme left. The quarry is out of view, behind the main house and slightly t
the left, where there was a sheer drop into the deep workings. (*Courtesy of George W. Cooke and Mrs Kathleen M. Robinson*

his view of the farm buildings and cottage attached to Rainborough Grange shows part of the large stack yard
n the left, the main yard in the centre and the bottom yard, which lies between the large building in the left
entre and the cottage on the right. Sam and Margaret Wake lived in the cottage during the Cookes' early
ccupancy of Rainborough Grange but moved during the Second World War. Sam Wake was a charge hand in the
oilers at nearby Cortonwood Colliery. John (Jack) Wake, their son, is still active in local politics, and was one-time
nayor of Barnsley.

Rainborough Grange when the Cooke family were in residence was a substantial, elegantly proportioned, four-
quare house, large enough to have several of its windows blocked up to avoid paying window tax. The house had
 plentiful water supply with mains water, spring water from a pump in the back kitchen and rainwater fed from a
ank in the roof. Mains electricity was not provided until 1955. The Cooke family moved to Rainborough Grange
om Ashton Farm, Brethwell, in 1939, succeeding the Cartwright family, and remained there until 1960: they
vere the last residents. The land was farmed by William Henry Cooke, his wife Hannah and their son George. The
'ookes' daughter Kathleen (now Mrs Robinson) was married from Rainborough Grange in 1959.

The site occupied by Rainborough Grange was known by some as Three Folds, on account of the three yards,
nd by others as Thief Hole, possibly a mispronunciation of Three Folds, or a name founded on legends which
rew surrounding the nearby quarry – a place where thieves could meet to share out their ill-gotten gains. The
nail coach ran from Barnsley to Worsborough Dale, passing through Dove Cliff, Jump, Hemingfield, Tingle Bridge
nd past Rainborough Grange towards the Cottage of Content. Stories abound about daring robberies near Thief
Iole Farm, one being that the highwayman who robbed the mail coach at Rainborough injured his leg during the
scapade. When Earl Fitzwilliam was seen limping the following day, it was rumoured that he had robbed the mail
oach himself.

Opencast mining, which took place nearby in 1943, mostly destroyed the natural springs, causing several
roblems on the Rainborough Grange estate. This was particularly noticeable during harsh winter weather, and in
he winter of 1947 eight weeks of frozen water caused a great deal of hardship.

The principal coach road to Rainborough Grange ran from New Road, more commonly called the Half-Mile Road, to the main yard. Turnips and mangel-wurzels were planted in the fields adjacent to the coach road during the 1950s. The coach road seen crossing in front of the farm buildings met Smithy Bridge Lane, just below Rainborough Lodge (also known as Lion's Lodge, or the Lion Gate).

The effects of opencast mining resulted in a gradual deterioration of the water supply and drainage on the Rainborough Grange estate. Farming the land was difficult. William Cooke's declining health meant that he was no longer able to assist his son George, so the Cookes decided to leave Rainborough Grange and moved to Snowdrop Farm, situated near the Old Church in Wentworth. Rainborough Grange stood empty, and from 1960 to 1967 the land was farmed by Mr Hoyle of West Melton, another tenant farmer on the Fitzwilliam (Wentworth) estates.

Opencast mining had created other problems as well. There was concern that Elsecar pit tip could subside and cause a major disaster, so it was decided to extend the tip and secure its extremities, where the threat of a landslide seemed most likely. The National Coal Board purchased Rainborough Grange and some of its land and the buildings were set on fire. The point of this is unclear, as all the buildings, the quarry and many fields were completely covered over by colliery waste. A mini mountain, originally an ugly purple and grey slag heap completely covers the site. Over a quarter of a century later the former waste tip is clad in a luscious green blanket. Rainborough Grange, with all its history, lies beneath. The site of the gateway marking the start of the coach road to Rainborough Grange can still be detected if one looks at the curb stones: travelling towards West Melton along the Half-Mile Road, about 75 yd from the end on the right-hand side the curb stones curve in marking the site where the gateposts stood until a few years ago. (*Courtesy of George W. Cooke and Mrs Kathleen M. Robinson*)

Rainborough Lodge from Smithy Bridge Lane in an early twentieth-century postcard view. Also known as the Lion Gate and more commonly as Lion's Lodge, this marks the entrance to Rainborough Park, and was built for William, 4th Earl Fitzwilliam, to the designs of John Carr in about 1796. (*George Hardy collection*)

The Radcliffe family outside the gamekeeper's cottage, Woodside (now known as Hemingfield Road), Wombwell, 1897. In the photograph are Margaret Radcliffe (known as Peggy), her husband Tom, and their seventeen-year-old son Robert. According to his granddaughter Edith, now Mrs Spencer, Tom Radcliffe came to the area from St Helens, hoping to find work. He had a wife and young family to support, and in 1880 he found himself in a spot of bother for poaching rabbits. The magistrate was impressed by Tom's manner and his plea that he was poaching only to ensure his family had meat on the table as, although willing to work, he had been unable to find suitable employment and had fallen on hard times. His previously unblemished record went in his favour, and the magistrate, Thomas Vernon-Wentworth, son of Frederick Vernon-Wentworth, of Wentworth Castle, clearly moved by Tom's circumstances, remarked 'I could do with a man like you working for me.' Following his court appearance Tom was offered a cottage, situated on the edge of the Wentworth estate in Wombwell Wood, seen here, and was employed as gamekeeper. (*Courtesy of Mrs Edith Spencer*)

Tom Radcliffe, gamekeeper, *c.* 1910.
(*Courtesy of Mrs Edith Spencer*)

Joseph Radcliffe, gamekeeper, son of Tom Radcliffe, seen here outside his home, the gamekeeper's cottage, Rockley Bottom, c. 1910. (*Courtesy of Mrs Edith Spencer*)

Joseph Radcliffe and his assistant raising pheasant chicks at Rockley Bottom, 1925. Like his father before him, Joseph Radcliffe worked for the Vernon-Wentworth family from Wentworth Castle. (*Courtesy of Mrs Edith Spencer*)

The old turnpike road (Sheffield Road), showing its junction with Broadcarr Road, 1970. On the right, beyond Wentworth station railway bridge, is Lidgett Garage. This was the former engine house of Lidgett Colliery. (*Joan Masheder collection*)

NCB Central Workshops, Birdwell, 1985, shortly before complete closure. Among some visitors to the works are Keith Bostwick (standing left), Alec Turner, and Harry Catlin (back right). (*Courtesy of Keith and Joan Bostwick*)

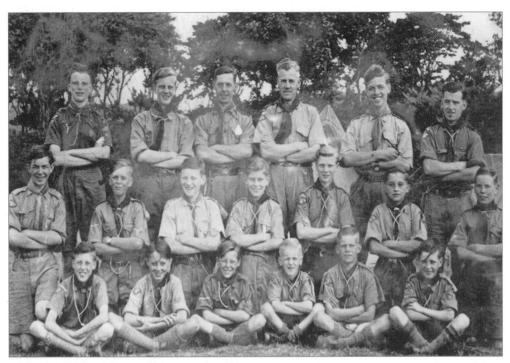

The Tankersley 4th Wentworth Scouts at Danes Dyke, Flamborough, *c.* 1949. Back row, left to right: Keith Bostwick, Jack Booker, Alf Keeling, Johnny Briggs (Scoutmaster), Master Jackson. Middle row: Jim Keeling, -?-, Eric Starkey, -?-, Geoffrey Booker, Peter Blackburn. Front row: the only identifiable scout is Hardy, third from the right. (*Courtesy of Keith and Joan Bostwick*)

Workers at the Wharncliffe Silkstone Colliery, sometimes referred to as Pilley Colliery, *c.* 1945. Among those featured in the photograph are Frank Money (standing left) and Rex Hague, who stands next to him. (*Courtesy of Peter Marsh and Margaret Marsh*)

The Joy Ride, Tankersley, 1920s. (*Walker's Newsagents collection*)

Mary Whitehouse (1918–1991), potato picking, somewhere in the Wentworth area, possibly at Pearson's Farm, 1930s. Mary picked potatoes at several farms in the area during that period. (*Margaret Gaddas collection*)

Locals pose outside the Royal Albert Hotel, Blacker Hill, 1936. Back row, left to right: Albert Armer, Mr Pollendine, Lambert Bissell, Ted Bissell, Herbert Mitchell (landlord), Joe Jevons, Steve Bissell, Joseph Bissell. Front row: Tommy Higgs, Bob Davison and Walt Smith (in flat cap, smoking pipe). (*Courtesy of Chris Thawley*)

Ladies' outing from Blacker Hill Working Men's Club, 1950s. Those pictured include Betty Guest, Winnie Morley, Mrs Yates, Madge White, Dora Charles, Betty Charles, Beatie Jones, Alice Waddington, Iris Ackroyd, Francis Davison, Mary Ackroyd, Mabel Foster, Mary Swallow, Jenny Gaunt, Martha Beckett, Elsie Hazlewood, Maggie Grant, Mrs Denton, Barbara Walker and Lillian Ackroyd. (*Courtesy of Iris Ackroyd*)

Blacker Hill Sunday School, *c.* 1954. Seated on the left is Mrs Firth, who in addition to teaching at the Sunday School was also schoolmistress at Blacker Hill Church of England School. Those pictured include Miss Hazlewood, Elaine Fowler, Pam Hazlewood, Barbara Dodson, Joy Dyson, Janet Hazlewood, Joy Grimshaw, Miss Fowler, Jennifer Bundy and Stuart Smith. (*Courtesy of Mrs Iris Ackroyd*)

Elizabethan pageant at Blacker Hill Church of England School, *c.* 1950. Robert Firth (son of the schoolmistress) is on the left and Frank Ackroyd is on the right. (*Courtesy of Mrs Iris Ackroyd*) .

Three pupils at Blacker Hill Church of England School tuck in to their Christmas pudding, December 1951. Le
right: Roger Allen, Yvonne Ackroyd, Janet Davison. (*Courtesy of Mrs Iris Ackroyd*)

Outside Blacker Hill Chapel, summer 1969
Left to right: Iris Ackroyd, Janice Wilson,
Victoria Ackroyd, Dot Bundy, Hazel (Dot's
niece), holding baby Deborah Wilson.
(*Courtesy of Mrs Iris Ackroyd*)

istmas party of High Green Sequence Dance, at High Green Welfare Hall, 1959. Left to right: Gertie Claydon, Mr Kay, Mrs Kay, Joan Bostwick, Keith Bostwick. (*Courtesy of Keith and Joan Bostwick*)

celebrated Cain and Abel statue was situated between
kley and Birdwell in the Old Park, which forms part of
Wentworth Estate at Stainborough. The residents of
itworth Castle were fond of statuary, obelisks and
es. Cain and Abel, as this popular statue was called
lly, seen here in the early 1900s, was made of lead.
statue was of two male figures wrestling and actually
esented Hercules and Antaeus. In the photograph one
re has an arm missing; by the 1940s the statue was
orted to be much damaged and vandalised. Articles in
Barnsley Chronicle in 1951 mention the statue's
ppearance, and the suspicion that it had been stolen.
rtesy of Chris Thawley)

ACKNOWLEDGEMENTS

My personal assistant John D. Murray, Mr Peter Marsh, whose notes on Upper Hoyland, Platts Common, Jump and various industrial sites throughout the area have proved invaluable. Mrs Margaret Marsh, Paul T. Langley Welch, Mr Herbert and Mrs Doreen Howse, Mr David and Mrs Christine Walker of Walker's Newsagents, Hoyland, Mr Clifford and Mrs Margaret Willoughby, Mrs Iris Ackroyd, Mr Keith Bostwick and Mrs Joan Bostwick, Mrs Ann Howse, Mr George Hardy, Graham Noble, Val Noble, Mrs Joan Hopson, Arthur K. Clayton BEM, Keith Hopkinson, Miss Suki B. Walker, Martin Johnson, Bob Mortimer, Keith Froggatt, Miss Sandra Hague, George W. Cooke, Mrs Kathleen M. Robinson, Guy Canby FRICS, Agent to the Fitzwilliam (Wentworth) Estates, Miss Tracy P. Deller, Master Ricki S. Deller, Miss Joanna C. Murray Deller, Les Gaddass, Margaret Gaddass, Mr Jack (John) Howse, Geoff Hazlewood JP, Mrs Mavis Foster, Sheila Margaret Ottley, Clarence Walker, Michael F. Bedford, Mr Maurice Jones, Chris Thawley of the Royal Albert Hotel, Blacker Hill, Brian Gash, Marlene Gash (née Bissell), Mrs Bissell, Mrs Christine Short, Sean David Lambe, Joan Masheder, Marion Brown, Mary Dickerson for her information about her grandfather Dr Barclay Wiggins, and father Dr Albert W. Barclay Wiggins, as well as information concerning fox hunting, Ronald Q. Dickerson, Rory Alexander Barclay Dickerson, Rose Willis, John Willis, Dot Peet, Sarah Mott, Mrs Sylvia Steel, Ralph Walker, Mrs Edith Spencer, Mrs Ivy Conway for her assistance in gathering material in the Upper Hoyland chapter, Brenda Loy, Mrs Phoebe R. Duggan, Mr E.A. Duggan, Mrs Isabelle Gillick, Mr John Richardson, Edwin Hugh Stenton and Amy Stenton, the late Doris Hague (former headmistress of Elsecar Church of England Infants' School), Mabel Shaw, Sue Jenkins, Carl Swift, Eric Todd, Cyril Slinn, Tony Briggs of Harvey and Richardson, Hoyland, Simon Fletcher, Michelle Tilling and Anne Bennett.

Paul T. Langley Welch, who has taken the present day photographs included in this book, works as a freelance commercial and theatrical photographer. Since 1983 he has been working for such companies as the National Theatre, the Old Vic and the Royal Shakespeare Company. Commercial clients include United Distillers, the National Tourist Board, the Arts Council of Great Britain, British Telecom and F1 Racing (Silverstone). He has also produced films in conjunction with Pauline Turner for PPM Productions, for the National Tourist Board; and photographed present-day views for *Around Hoyland* and *Sheffield Past & Present*, also by Geoffrey Howse.